New York

A Bicentennial History

Bruce Bliven, Jr.

W. W. Norton & Company, Inc.
New York

American Association for State and Local History
Nashville

Copyright © 1981
American Association for State and Local History
Nashville, Tennessee

Published and distributed by
W. W. Norton & Company, Inc.
500 Fifth Avenue
New York, New York 10110

Library of Congress Cataloguing-in-Publication Data

Bliven, Bruce, 1916–
New York, a Bicentennial history.

(The States and the Nation series)
Bibliography: p.
Includes index.
1. New York (State)—History. I. Title.
II. Series: States and the Nation series.
F119.B69   974.7   80-26246
ISBN 0–393–05665–1

Printed in the United States of America

1 2 3 4 5 6 7 8 9 0

To Naomi and Fred

Contents

Illustrations

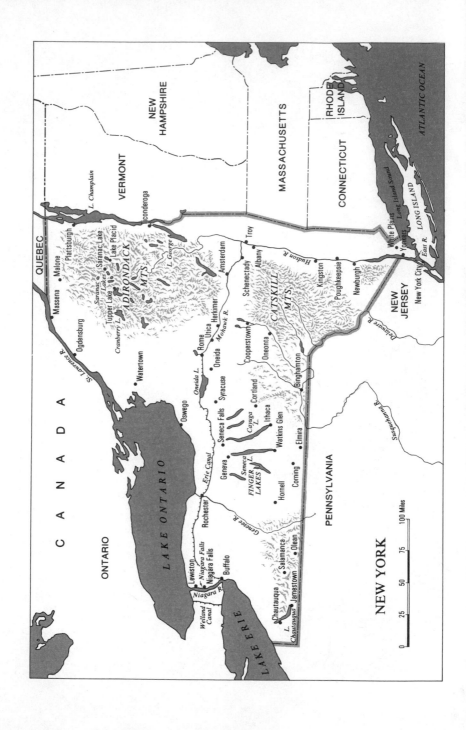

Invitation to the Reader

IN 1807, former President John Adams argued that a complete history of the American Revolution could not be written until the history of change in each state was known, because the principles of the Revolution were as various as the states that went through it. Two hundred years after the Declaration of Independence, the American nation has spread over a continent and beyond. The states have grown in number from thirteen to fifty. And democratic principles have been interpreted differently in every one of them.

We therefore invite you to consider that the history of your state may have more to do with the bicentennial review of the American Revolution than does the story of Bunker Hill or Valley Forge. The Revolution has continued as Americans extended liberty and democracy over a vast territory. John Adams was right: the states are part of that story, and the story is incomplete without an account of their diversity.

The Declaration of Independence stressed life, liberty, and the pursuit of happiness; accordingly, it shattered the notion of holding new territories in the subordinate status of colonies. The Northwest Ordinance of 1787 set forth a procedure for new states to enter the Union on an equal footing with the old. The Federal Constitution shortly confirmed this novel means of building a nation out of equal states. The step-by-step process through which territories have achieved self-government and national representation is among the most important of the Founding Fathers' legacies.

The method of state-making reconciled the ancient conflict between liberty and empire, resulting in what Thomas Jefferson called an empire for liberty. The system has worked and remains unaltered, despite enormous changes that have taken

ix

place in the nation. The country's extent and variety now sur-
pass anything the patriots of '76 could likely have imagined.
The United States has changed from an agrarian republic into a
highly industrial and urban democracy, from a fledgling nation
into a major world power. As Oliver Wendell Holmes remarked
in 1920, the creators of the nation could not have seen completely how it and its constitution and its states would develop.
Any meaningful review in the bicentennial era must consider
what the country has become, as well as what it was.

The new nation of equal states took as its motto *E Pluribus
Unum*—"out of many, one." But just as many peoples have
become Americans without complete loss of ethnic and cultural
identities, so have the states retained differences of character.
Some have been superficial, expressed in stereotyped images—
big, boastful Texas, "sophisticated" New York, "hillbilly"
Arkansas. Other differences have been more real, sometimes instructively, sometimes amusingly; democracy has embraced
Huey Long's Louisiana, bilingual New Mexico, unicameral Ne-
braska, and a Texas that once taxed fortunetellers and spawned
politicians called "Woodpecker Republicans" and "Skunk
Democrats." Some differences have been profound, as when
South Carolina secessionists led other states out of the Union in
opposition to abolitionists in Massachusetts and Ohio. The result was a bitter Civil War.

The Revolution's first shots may have sounded in Lexington
and Concord; but fights over what democracy should mean and
who should have independence have erupted from Pennsylvania's Gettysburg to the "Bleeding Kansas" of John Brown,
from the Alamo in Texas to the Indian battles at Montana's
Little Bighorn. Utah Mormons have known the strain of isolation; Hawaiians at Pearl Harbor, the terror of attack; Georgians
during Sherman's march, the sadness of defeat and devastation.
Each state's experience differs instructively; each adds understanding to the whole.

The purpose of this series of books is to make that kind of understanding accessible, in a way that will last in value far
beyond the bicentennial fireworks. The series offers a volume
on every state, plus the District of Columbia—fifty-one, in all.

Each book contains, besides the text, a view of the state through eyes other than the author's—a "photographer's essay," in which a skilled photographer presents his own personal perceptions of the state's contemporary flavor.

We have asked authors not for comprehensive chronicles, nor for research monographs or new data for scholars. Bibliographies and footnotes are minimal. We have asked each author for a summing up—interpretive, sensitive, thoughtful, individual, even personal—of what seems significant about his or her state's history. What distinguishes it? What has mattered about it, to its own people and to the rest of the nation? What has it come to now?

To interpret the states in all their variety, we have sought a variety of backgrounds in authors themselves and have encouraged variety in the approaches they take. They have in common only these things: historical knowledge, writing skill, and strong personal feelings about a particular state. Each has wide latitude for the use of the short space. And if each succeeds, it will be by offering you, in your capacity as a *citizen* of a state *and* of a nation, stimulating insights to test against your own.

James Morton Smith
General Editor

New York

1

On Finding New York

*M*Y study of New York history began on roller skates. My skates had metal—not plastic—wheels, and leather ankle straps, and, at their toe ends, metal clamps that fitted on the edges of the soles of my shoes. I wore a skate key on a string around my neck. With that key, according to the directions, I could tighten the clamps so firmly that there was no danger of my skates separating from my shoes just as I was getting up to my top speed. The directions were wrong. It was not my falling down that mattered so much, however, as *where* I fell: on Claremont Avenue, a short street tucked in between Riverside Drive and Broadway just west of the Columbia University campus on Manhattan's Upper West Side.

In a year or two, I had come to know the feel of Claremont Avenue from 116th Street to 120th Street. It took me a quarter of a century to realize that Claremont Avenue and the streets in its vicinity crisscross the main battlefield in the action in front of Harlem Heights on September 16, 1776—a medium-sized battle of considerable psychological significance. By that time I had begun to read some early American history, mostly out of a sense of embarrassment at having been graduated from high school, college, and officer candidate school without being exposed to the subject beyond a tenth-grade civics course. Although I was considerably interested in government, economics, and current affairs, I tended to think that nothing worth men-

3

tioning had happened before the First World War. But in Douglas Southall Freeman's magnificent *George Washington* I discovered that I had learned to roller skate on hallowed ground. The map of the battle action, reproduced from H. P. Johnston's *The Battle of Harlem Heights* (1897), amazed and delighted me: the "Main Action in 'Buckwheat Field,' 12:00 to 1:00 PM" had taken place on the very place my wheels knew best.

It was not far from the buckwheat field to the larger story of New York City and New York Province in the War of the Revolution as a whole, which led backward in time to New York before the Revolution and from there to New York before the English. Since it was hard to avoid wondering how things worked out after independence had been won, the trail also led irresistibly in the opposite direction, forward in time. I soon learned the one incontrovertible fact about New York history: the student runs no danger of running out of reading material.

Roller skates are more popular transportation for all ages now that they come with shoes attached, like ice skates, and cannot come unclamped. I must take it for granted that American history will grow in popularity. Much of historic New York that cannot be skated conveniently can be walked or bicycled or driven through, and an astonishingly large part of where things happened in New York State is approachable by water. A visit to almost any one of its historic sites proves that in one way or another large numbers of people—New Yorkers, former New Yorkers, and total strangers—are looking for New York history and finding it. A substantial number of our relics of the past are preserved, polished, labeled, and starred invitingly in the travel guide books.

The National Park Service maintains a spread of notable places including the Saratoga battlefield, Franklin D. Roosevelt's Hyde Park home, Theodore Roosevelt's birthplace on Manhattan (as well as his summer home, Sagamore Hill, at Oyster Bay and the Wilcox House in Buffalo where he took the presidential oath of office in 1901), Fort Stanwix, the Schuyler Mansion in Schuylerville, the Statue of Liberty, Castle Clinton, Hamilton's Grange, and Federal Hall on Wall Street in New York City. The state takes care of many more historic sites: the

Schuyler Mansion in Albany, Fort Crailo in Rensselaer, Fort Ontario in Oswego, and the Oriskany battlefield, six miles east of Rome, to mention just a few. The State Museum at the south end of the Nelson A. Rockefeller Plaza in Albany is a model of up-to-date exhibit techniques. And there are hundreds more places where New York history is presented invitingly in preservations, restorations, recreations, memorials, and exhibitions organized by historical societies, counties, cities, towns, villages, and private entrepreneurs: the South Street Seaport, the Whaling Museum at Sag Harbor, Long Island, the Huguenot Street Old Stone Houses in New Paltz, Susan B. Anthony's house in Rochester, Washington's headquarters in White Plains, Philipsburg Manor in North Tarrytown, Fort Ticonderoga on Lake Champlain (with Mt. Hope, Mt. Defiance, and Mt. Independence in the near distance).

Of course, all of New York is historic in some sense, even if you have to ignore what is there for the time being. I must confess to a wayward delight in detecting history in places where it has not achieved official recognition, and I live in the ideal place for that pleasure. My home base, Manhattan, had always been too concerned about the future to waste time on its past. Anything very old has customarily been seen as an object very ripe for demolition. The landmarks-preservation people are fighting against that commercial assumption with some success; but the wreckers, moving in ahead of the builders, win the lion's share of all but the most highly publicized arguments. I take pleasure in seeing the past win its occasional victories, even though I root hard for the future of the city as a whole— which doubtless means, as the builders argue, further additions to the massive blanket of brick, concrete, and asphalt that has already been spread over the island.

The ground retains a certain shape despite the fillings-in and the flattenings-out. One may think of Manhattan as flat, but not many of its streets are truly level for more than a few blocks at a stretch. With a pinch of imagination one can remove the fill, restore the crests of the hills, plant a profusion of oak, pine, walnut, chestnut, and maple trees, and recreate the rolling, boulder-strewn landscape that the Reckagawanancs—the Algonquian

tribe that lived in what are now Riverdale and Yonkers—
regarded as an excellent hunting ground. (The Algonquian word
"manah" means "island" and "atin" means "hill"; thus
"manahatin," "hilly island.")

In Dutch days the island was well watered by streams,
brooks, spring-fed ponds, and marshes; and although nearly all
the water has been driven underground, the springs are irre-
pressible. Countless buildings are compelled to keep pumps
going all or part of the time in order to keep their basements
dry. In parts of the island, whenever an excavation for a new
building is dug, an old stream—Minetta Brook, for instance, in
the vicinity of Washington Square—seeps in and attempts to fill
up the hole with fresh water while the contractors gnash their
teeth with irritation.

A walk through Central Park can give the imagination-game
player priceless clues to the past, despite the artistry with which
Frederick Law Olmsted and Calvert Vaux worked, in 1857, to
improve upon nature. I am especially fond of Central Park's
massive gray rock outcroppings. They are lined on top with
well-defined grooves, parallel because of their glacial origin.
Twenty-five thousand years ago, as the great icecap that spread
over North America advanced about as far as it was going, these
grooves were ground out by rocks at the bottom of the glacier
that had been pushed slowly south under the weight of one
thousand feet of ice above them. The ice moved as far south as
Staten Island and stopped. When it melted, it left terminal
moraine—the mass of gravel, rocks, sand, dirt, and debris it
had accumulated—to form the ridge that runs from Tottenville
to the western end of the Verrazano Bridge and then across
Brooklyn and a long way to the east on Long Island.

The icecap covered almost all of New York State except for a
small area in the west, in Chautauqua and Cattaraugus counties.
It deepened valleys, rounded hills, and formed the thousands of
lakes. It redirected brooks and streams, creating waterfalls and
rapids. The coastal plain submerged and water filled the low-
lands, and Staten Island, Manhattan, and Long Island became
separate entities. On the south side of the terminal moraine,
sand from the melting glacier created a low-lying outwash,
forming Sandy Hook, Coney Island, and Rockaway.

So, to my mind, the grooves in the Central Park rocks are a kind of ideogram: the secret of the history of New York is geography and geology. New York history needed a superlative natural harbor at the mouth of a great river that would lead to a river valley breaking the mountain barrier and pointing the way to the Great Lakes and the west. The glacier put all that into shape and almost gratuitously added in Lake George, which nearly connects to Lake Champlain, which leads north via the Richelieu River to the St. Lawrence. This pattern of rivers, lakes, and valleys—a great T-formation tipped forward on its side—has been intimately involved with virtually all the events of the past three hundred fifty years, since the arrival of Europeans, as well as for the five or six thousand years before that, after the first Paleo-Indian hunters arrived.

The Algonquians, including the Mohicans, Delawares, Wappingers, Montauks, and others, began to occupy New York about 1000 A.D. The Iroquois, including the Erie, Seneca, Cayuga, Huron, Onondaga, Mohawk, and Oneida tribes, followed in about the year 1300—unless, as one school of archaeologists argues, there were Iroquois in the Finger Lakes district much earlier than that. The Indians, like the later Dutch and English pioneers, settled near water, whether ocean, sound, river, or lake. Until the Revolution, the rivers and the river valleys channeled the course of New York history; during the Revolution, they dictated British strategy; after the Revolution they became even more influential.

Now that the nation's Bicentennial has been celebrated (merely its *beginning,* as I insist in a churlish tone of voice, since the anniversary of the end of the fighting, at Yorktown, is October 19, 1981, and the anniversary of the signing of the Treaty of Paris is September 3, 1983), New Yorkers, like the citizens of all the other states, may feel that they have had a surfeit of self-congratulation. I felt that New York's Bicentennial effort was muted—at any rate, the small part of it that I observed. The great exception was New York City's explosion of good will on July 4, 1976, when the Tall Ships—ocean-going sailing vessels from all over the world—sailed through the harbor and as far north as the George Washington Bridge. At the time, both city and state were in appalling financial difficulties—far worse, I think, than the average New Yorker found credible. Perhaps it was psychologically impossible for New York to rejoice in full measure over the two centuries of troubles that it had survived.

By something more than coincidence, New York City's reaction to the Declaration of Independence two hundred years earlier was also muted. The full text arrived in New York from Philadelphia on July 9, 1776, following the Continental Congress's vote of approval on July 4. George Washington's entire army, with just a few exceptions, was assembled on Manhattan, Governor's Island, and Brooklyn Heights, and the British had already landed. General William Howe's powerful expeditionary force, outnumbering the Americans by about two to one, had taken possession of Staten Island a week earlier. The entire lower harbor was filled with the warships and transports, nearly three hundred in number, that were supporting the invasion. New York understood perfectly well that the British could move on from Staten Island whenever they chose and land almost anywhere that suited their purpose.

At six o'clock on the evening of the 9th, on Washington's order, the Declaration was read to all the American brigades in formation at their various posts. The largest group of soldiers was on the Manhattan parade ground, the Commons, the open space that with some slight trimming now forms City Hall Park. Washington wanted every man in his command to hear "the grounds and reasons" for the war, as the Continental Congress had expressed them (a little late, perhaps, since the fighting had been going on for almost fifteen months). Washington and his aides were present at the reading on the Commons, and so were a good many New York civilians, who formed a crowd around the edges of the parade ground and spilled over into the adjacent streets. They were close enough to hear the words as one of the general's aides shouted them out.

In Philadelphia and Baltimore, where the Declaration had already been read aloud, the public reaction had been jubilant, with bonfires, gunshots, and cannon fire added to the crowd's cheering. New York's response was very different. The civilian observers were quiet. After the soldiers' formation had been dismissed, a good many of the New Yorkers, together with some of the soldiers who did not have to report immediately for guard duty, walked down Broadway toward the Battery. New Yorkers liked bonfires and in the past had lit them on the Commons at every slight excuse; but that night a bonfire or the boom of a cannon or pealing church bells might have been misinterpreted as a signal that the British attack had begun. A sizable crowd of strollers accumulated at Bowling Green, at the south end of Broadway, as it did on every pleasant evening before curfew. The crowd was larger than usual—soldiers, civilian men, women, children—but its mood seemed about the same as on an ordinary night.

New Yorkers had been collecting every scrap of lead that they could find as part of the city's belated campaign to improve its own defenses: lead to melt and mold into bullets and shot. Someone, remembering that the equestrian statue of King George III that stood in the grassy oval in the center of Bowling Green was made of gilded lead, realized that the lead-collection committee had overlooked a treasure. A party of agile young men with ropes and crowbars climbed the marble pedestal that supported the statue. They pulled and pried until it toppled over. It crashed to the ground—it was said to weigh four thousand pounds—and cracked in several places. A man with a crowbar jimmied off the king's head. Even that symbolic act did not arouse cheers, a fact that surprised the captain of one of the Pennsylvania companies who thought the New Yorkers seemed strangely cold and indifferent. He may not have understood that they were wholly intent on getting lead—not demonstrating, or expressing rage, but working hard to improve their slim chance of keeping New York City out of the enemy's hands.

There are children who seem to have established who they are going to be the rest of their lives by about the time they are old enough to crawl (to the profound frustration, in some cases, of parents, grandparents, teachers, and psychologists with ambitions to shape the infant's personality toward their own definitions of what would be desirable). I find that New York is like one of those children. An analogy between a state and a child, I tell myself, is outrageously unscientific; yet the similarities between old New York—as it was, let's say, in 1700—and present-day New York are tantalizing. For instance, at an early age New York was distinctly not admired by the twelve other colonies; when New Yorkers were criticized, which was constantly, they seemed to shrug off all complaints with irritating complacence as if to show scorn for the comments of anyone with the poor judgment to live in another province. Since New Yorkers disagreed among themselves about nearly everything, they criticized themselves unstintingly, which was about as annoying as seeming not to care. If Williamsburg, Virginia, held New York City in low esteem, Williamsburg's opinions were probably mild compared to the things that were being said in Albany or on the eastern end of Long Island. New York possessed a great harbor and a prospering port town that was senior to its chief rivals, Boston, Philadelphia, Baltimore, and Charleston. But it did not win the respect that supposedly is due seniority.

During this past decade, New York has become self-conscious about its reputation, worried—with reason—about its credit rating, and fearful that more companies may move out of the state. The state Department of Commerce has taken to advertising New York in papers like the *Wall Street Journal:* "Introducing The New And Improved New York." But that is very new. Most of the time, through the centuries, New York has let its reputation take care of itself and ignored external criticism while continuing the internal. New Yorkers have been fully occupied along other lines, looking for profitable innovations in every field of human endeavor, especially business and finance. Most of what they found has been passed along to the rest of the country, often with a New Yorker, or a group of New Yorkers, moving west or south or southwest along with the new technique. New York has set styles in every field, from government to banking, from publishing to television, in crime as well as in ballet. Despite its problems, it continues to do so.

2

Early Exploration and Permanent Settlement

f one takes permanent settlement by Europeans as the starting point, New York State history began in the spring of 1624 when the Dutch West India Company's ship *Nieu Nederlandt* dropped off small parties of colonists at the future sites of New York City and Albany. For one hundred years before that, to be sure, Europe had known about the area. Explorers had found the remarkable natural harbor and the broad river that flowed into it and had taken the news home, and quite a few temporary settlements or encampments had been established. But the colony on the southern tip of Manhattan Island was the first that lasted.

In April 1524—just thirty-two years after Columbus had discovered the New World—Giovanni da Verrazano, an Italian navigator–captain working for King Francis I of France, came upon the bay. Like Columbus, and many of the other explorers that followed, Verrazano was trying to find a passage to the Orient. He was afraid to sail his ship *Dauphine* through the Narrows, which the Verrazano Bridge now crosses, because he had already lost three of the four ships he had started with and the danger of running aground was appalling. Verrazano did take the *Dauphine*'s small boat through the Narrows, however, and saw the bay, which looked to him like "a most beautiful lake." Indians came down to the shores to watch, and Verrazano counted thirty or forty Indian canoes on the water. But before the small boat had gone far, "a violent contrary wind" blew in

11

from the sea and forced the party to return to the *Dauphine*.
In his letter–report to the king, Verrazano wrote: "We found
a pleasant situation among some little steep hills, through which
a very large river forced its way to the sea." Since the tidal nature of the lower Hudson confused quite a few later explorers
into thinking that it might be a strait, not a river, and possibly a
passage to the Orient, Verrazano's correct identification is impressive. If the tide had been coming in, and the river had
seemed to be flowing north, Verrazano might not have been so
casual about leaving the lower bay. He sailed east along the
south shore of Long Island "greatly regretting to leave this
region," as he wrote, because it "seemed so commodious and
delightful, and which we supposed must contain great riches."
Still, the Narrows did not lead to China, which disappointed
Francis I as much as it did Verrazano, and the French did
nothing to consolidate Verrazano's discovery claim.

Conceivably other explorers saw the New York harbor before
Verrazano. The list includes the Norseman Leif, son of Eric the
Red; the Englishman John Cabot; the Italian Amerigo Vespucci;
and a few others. In every case the evidence for discovery
before 1524 is vague, and in Leif Ericsson's case the "Vin-
land" he found was L'Anse aux Meadows, Newfoundland. The
evidence for Verrazano's claim, on the other hand, could hardly
be better: his letter–report to Francis I with accompanying maps
drawn by Verrazano's brother was convincing evidence that
he had seen what he had seen.

Through the rest of the sixteenth century, quite a few other
men found the bay and river. Estéban Gomez, a Portuguese
black working for King Charles of Spain, sailed through the
Narrows into the upper bay in January 1526. Gomez decided
against trying to sail up the river because it was clogged with
ice floes. In 1534, the Frenchman Jacques Cartier explored the
St. Lawrence River as far west as present-day Montreal; and
about 1540 French traders constructed a small fort near the site
of what is now Albany. (There is a map in Paris, dated 1570,
that shows the mouth of the Hudson in considerable detail.)

Decades later, another Frenchman entered what is now New
York with a purpose other than exploration. Samuel de Cham-

plain, Frenchman *extraordinaire,* had established the fur-trade post of Port Royale in present Nova Scotia in 1604. Four years later, after scouting the New England coast as far south as the southern coast of Cape Cod in search of a better site for his enterprise, he established a new post at Quebec. Champlain truly was an extraordinary man: talented, brave, moral, and also likable. He played politics with the Indians of the St. Lawrence valley—notably, helping them fight the Iroquois and especially the Mohawk—and entered the lake that would bear his name on July 12, 1609, not to explore but to fight with an alliance of Huron, Algonquin, and Montagnais against the Mohawk.

If in retrospect Europe seems to have been slow in appreciating the value of New York real estate, Spain's successes in Central and South America were partly to blame. Spain had quickly seized the regions most capable of returning quick profits: the Caribbean islands, Mexico and the Aztec empire, and Peru and the Inca empire. Gold and silver treasure went a long way toward making up for the disappointment of not finding a short route to China. Under Charles V and his son, Philip II, who succeeded Charles in 1556, Spain seemed almost too powerful to challenge in either the New World or the Old. But before the century ended, and most dramatically after the English defeat of Philip's Armada in 1588, that changed. The English were claiming most of the east coast of North America— everything that Queen Elizabeth's favorite, Sir Walter Raleigh, had explored—and calling all of it "Virginia"; in 1607 the London Company, with a grant from King James I, founded Jamestown, the first permanent English colony in the New World.

Meanwhile the Dutch, who had begun their rebellion against Spain in 1565, had organized as the United Netherlands in 1571 and had arranged a truce in 1609. The Dutch East India Company, looking for a quicker and safer route to China, organized an expedition to search for one and hired an Englishman, Henry Hudson, to command it. The Company supplied Hudson with a seventy-ton ship, the *Half Moon;* a crew of eighteen; and a guarantee of eight hundred guilders' pay, plus an additional two hundred for his wife in case he failed to return. Dutch geographers believed that there was a northeast passage to the Indies, if one could crash an ice barrier in the Barents Sea, and Hudson sailed as far as Novaya Zemlya. The ice was too formidable, and his crew grew mutinous, so Hudson decided instead to look for a northwest passage that might or might not begin 4,300 miles to the southwest. His friend Captain John Smith of Virginia had mentioned it to Hudson: "a sea leading into the western ocean, by the north of the southern English colony."

On September 2, 1609, Hudson anchored in the lower bay, off Sandy Hook, and ten days later he sailed the *Half Moon* through the Narrows ("a good entrance between two headlands"). He sailed up the river—Hudson called it "The Great River of the Mountain"—for seventeen days, mostly drifting on the incoming tides and then anchoring when the river flowed souih. That took the *Half Moon* almost to present-day Albany; Hudson dared not go north of a place where the river was only seven feet deep. Undoubtedly he had realized earlier that he was not on a sea leading into the western ocean, but to make absolutely certain he sent the small boat on upstream as far as it could go in half a day. The mate of the small boat returned with the bad news: it was a river.

While visions of spices, silks, and pearls had to be put aside, Hudson was greatly impressed by the river and the river's valley. He had gone ashore several times and had been entertained by friendly Indians, and he had allowed Indians to visit the *Half Moon* (at about the same time Champlain and the Algonquin were fighting the Mohawk). Their abundance of fruits, vegetables, skins, and furs was noted, and a most important piece of information was acquired: the Indians were more than willing to trade what they had, including beaver skins, for trinkets. Hudson's experience with the Indians was not all good. Almost at the outset, before the river exploration, the crew of the small boat had fought with Indians, and Hudson's lieutenant, John Colman, had been killed by an arrow wound in his throat. Then Hudson had kidnapped two Indians and locked them up aboard the *Half Moon*. The second event had nothing to do with the first, though it looked like reprisal. Hudson intended to take the

Indians back to Amsterdam as souvenirs of his adventure in conformity with the cruel custom of explorers at the time. On the way downriver the two Indian prisoners escaped, got ashore, and formed a war party of perhaps one hundred braves. The Indians attacked the *Half Moon* at the Highlands—where the Bear Mountain Bridge now crosses the river—and fought a losing battle with Hudson's crew all the way down to the bay.

Henry Hudson left his river on October 4 and put in at Dartmouth, England, thirty-four days later, but he never did get back to Amsterdam. The English felt that Hudson had betrayed his country and his king, James I, by working for the Dutch, and they refused to let him finish his voyage. The *Half Moon,* under another captain but without Hudson's journals and maps, which the English had confiscated, went on to Amsterdam months later. Hudson wrote the East India Company in an effort to convince its directors that he had found something valuable, but most of them did not agree. In their eyes a Great River that led next to nowhere was simply an expensive disappointment. (Hudson himself suffered a terrible fate. He attempted another polar passage exploration, this time working for the English. His crew mutinied in June 1611, put Hudson and his son into a small boat, and cast them adrift somewhere near Newfoundland. They were never seen again.)

Some Dutch businessmen, including a few members of the East India Company, warmed to Hudson's report and (undoubtedly aware of French success in Canada) sensed that trading with the Indians for furs might prove highly profitable. Throughout the next decade, Dutch traders were busy proving that point. In a single year, 1613, five Dutch traders crossed the Atlantic—including Adrien Block in the *Tiger* and Hendrick Christiaensz in the *Fortuyn.* Block explored Long Island Sound, where he named one small island for himself, and sailed up the Hudson as far as he could go. On what is now Castle Island, not far south of Albany, Block built a small redoubt and named it Fort Nassau. Supposedly it was built on the remains of the strongpoint the French had built in 1540. Block and Christiaensz got home with a wealth of furs and a much improved map, and their company, the United New Netherland Company, was awarded the right to make four more trading trips during the next three years.

Meanwhile a new venture, the West India Company, was being formed. It had a bigger idea: it planned to colonize New Netherland by establishing permanent settlements of farmers and their families who were brave enough, or desperate enough, to be the pioneers. They could deal with the Indians all year long, develop the fertile land, build towns, exercise government and administer justice, and thus challenge any assertion by any other European power—Spain, in particular—that New Netherland was not Dutch. In 1621 the charter for the West India Company was complete; in 1623 New Netherland was formally designated as a province of the Company; and in 1624 the first party of official settlers, divided into four groups, was ashore.

The boundaries of New Netherland were not clear, since the question was how much you could get away with, but in the Dutch view it included everything between the Delaware and Connecticut rivers with the Hudson at about the middle of the bite. There were some thirty families on board the *Nieu Nederlandt,* and most of them were not Dutch but Walloons—French-speaking Huguenots from what is now part of southwestern Belgium who had fled from Catholic France to escape persecution for their Protestant faith.

The captain of the ship, Cornelis Jacobsz Mey, put eight men on what is now Governor's Island, off the southern tip of Manhattan, on the theory that if the Indians were not friendly the advance party could defend itself more easily on the smaller island. There were wild walnut and chestnut trees growing there in abundance, so the settlers called it "Nooten" or "Nut" Island, a name that survived for more than one hundred fifty years. A few weeks later, Captain Mey took a slightly larger group, including four married couples, up the Hudson to Fort Nassau, which had fallen apart in the ten-year interval, and got the reconstruction work started. (When the new redoubt was finished it was renamed Fort Orange.) The third group went to the Delaware and on its eastern bank, in what is now Gloucester, just south of Philadelphia–Camden, began another fort eventually named Fort Nassau. The fourth group—two families and six extra men—went up the Fresh River, now the Connecticut, to a site not far from present-day Hartford. The four-settlements plan looked better on a map back at the West India Company's headquarters than it did on the ground; still, the earliest reports from New Netherland were fairly promising.

At the end of three months, a second ship brought another forty-five Walloons, furniture, cooking utensils, farm equipment, and more than one hundred head of livestock—cattle, sheep, horses, and fat Dutch hogs. By the end of a year the population of the Manhattan Island colony had grown to nearly two hundred, including slaves. West India Company engineers in the home office, working from a map, had planned New Amsterdam in remarkable detail: the exact design of the fort, the pattern of the streets, the location of the church and the school. The settlers complied with the blueprints as best they could with some optimism. They had promised to stay for six years unless the Company decided to move them elsewhere, and most of them expected to keep their bargain. They were risking their very lives, but they thought they would survive the weather, hunger, disease, and the possibility of trouble with the Indians. As it turned out, most of the settlers were right.

The Dutch ruled New Netherland for only forty years. In September 1664, Governor Peter Stuyvesant reluctantly surrendered the territory to the British, who had never admitted in writing that the Dutch claim was any good. King Charles II had made a present of it to his brother James, Duke of York; and so Fort Amsterdam became Fort James and New Amsterdam became New-York. On English maps New Netherland appeared as two and one-half provinces—New York, New Jersey, and the western part of Connecticut. The wonder was that the Dutch, in so short a time, made such a great impression on the New York part of their claim, on the town, the river valley, and the whole province.

As a byproduct of the on-again, off-again war with England, the Dutch regained title to New York for one additional year, 1673–74, which meant that all the place names got changed another time. New-York town became New Orange in honor of

Holland's new head of state and England's future king, William of Orange. And then, by the terms of the peace treaty that ended the war in 1674, the English got the province back and New Orange was called New-York, as before.

The settlers created a reality that far outlasted the vagaries of the wars in Europe. Although the fur trade was all that had interested the West India Company, nearly all of the settlers were farmers, not fur traders. The fur trade was handled by a few Company agents, and it took comparatively little time. The farmers needed acreage for wheat, rye, barley, oats, beans, peas, cabbages, melons, and flax and for their apple and cherry orchards. In less than forty years they were farming on cleared land throughout what are now the city's five boroughs and beyond and establishing place names that are still in use, with their spellings slightly changed, like Breuckelen (Brooklyn), Vlissingen (Flushing), Roode Hoeck (Red Hook), and many more.

The spreading-out process was assisted by Dutch religious toleration. From the beginning New Netherland had had an established religion, by order of the West India Company's directors. The Dutch Reformed Church included in the original plans was the only church building in New Amsterdam for quite a time, but the Company had not believed that men and women should be compelled to worship in the established way and the settlers agreed with it. Perhaps half of the New Amsterdam population did not attend the Dutch Reformed services. When New England Puritans were persecuting non-Puritans in the 1630s and 1640s, New Netherland was a haven for the victims. They were allowed to buy land and build churches of their own. The Reverend John Throckmorton, an Anabaptist, arrived from Salem, Massachusetts, with thirty-five like-minded families, and settled in what is now the East Bronx on land that included present-day Throg's Neck. Anne Hutchinson, banished from Boston, settled with her children and some of her disciples at Pelham Neck, near what is now New Rochelle. The Reverend Francis Doughty and several associates built a reformed Christian Church and founded Newtown, a village on the creek that empties into the East River, part of the boundary between Queens and Brooklyn. Another refugee from Salem, Lady

3

An English Province

OR all its diversity, the colony was unmistakably Dutch in 1664. The striking exception was the eastern end of Long Island: towns like Southampton, East Hampton, and Southold, which had first been settled by Puritans from Connecticut in 1640, were clearly English. In forty years the population had grown to perhaps 9,000, New York City—the settlement at the southern tip of Manhattan Island, that is—to about 1,500. There were farms throughout what are today the other four boroughs of the city, in the present-day suburbs, and up both sides of the Hudson River valley. About three hundred people lived in the town of Albany (as Beverwyck, formerly Fort Orange, had been named).

The rate of population growth had been increasing because the Dutch, who were forever changing the rules, had made the requirements for a patroonship less ambitious and had reduced the size of the land grants accordingly. In 1629, a qualified entrepreneur who brought at least fifty tenant-farmers to New Netherland at his own expense had been awarded a vast tract of land for their settlement. He had been able to choose between eighteen miles of Hudson River waterfront property on one side and nine miles along both sides, with no limit on how far the boundaries might extend east or west. But fifty willing tenants fifteen years old or older had not been easy to find and the total expense of, in effect, establishing a sub-colony within the col-

Deborah Moody, settled with a group of dissenters near Gravesend Bay, now the Bensonhurst section of Brooklyn.

The autocratic Stuyvesant, who governed New Netherland for the last seventeen of the forty years of Dutch control, did his mean-spirited best to subvert the Company's tolerant policy. Stuyvesant, the son of a minister and a soldier by profession, was prejudiced against almost anyone who did not belong to the Dutch Reformed Church; his special antipathies were toward Jews, Quakers, and Lutherans. When he arrived to take command, New Amsterdam was disorderly, even for a seaport. Stuyvesant imagined that he could run it like a military garrison, with a strong emphasis on discipline. He favored religious conformity if mostly for the sake of orderliness.

The Company, on the other hand, wanted more settlers. Its permissiveness, while right in step with Holland's viewpoint at the time, was commercial rather than theological. If a settler could be found, the Company directors did not want him disqualified on religious grounds. If a tolerant attitude attracted pioneers, well and good. The first Jews arrived in 1654—a few from Holland first, and then a group of twenty-three, mostly Spanish or Portuguese originally, who had fled to Holland from their native lands and had then been sent to Brazil as West India Company colonists. They had been driven out of Brazil by the Portuguese, who took over from the Dutch. The twenty-three took it for granted that they would be welcome in the West India Company's New Amsterdam. On the contrary, as soon as Stuyvesant understood that they meant to settle there he wrote an immoderate letter asking the Company to recall them and to stop sending Jews to New Netherland altogether. Stuyvesant's minister, Johannes Megapolensis, who had served first up the Hudson at Rensselaerswyck, seconded Stuyvesant's complaint: "We have here Papists, Mennonites and Lutherans among the Dutch, also many Puritans or Independents and many atheists and various other servants of Baäl . . . it would create still greater confusion, if the obstinate and immovable Jews came to settle here."[1]

---

1. Quoted in Henri and Barbara Van der Zee, *A Sweet and Alien Land* (New York: Viking Press, 1978), p. 291.

The Company was completely out of sympathy with the Stuyvesant–Megapolensis argument. Its directors were convinced that Jewish settlers could help New Netherland as they had helped the United Netherlands since 1605, when the Jews had been allowed to establish their first congregation in Amsterdam. Moreover, the Company did not intend to insult the small but valued number—perhaps 4 percent—of shareholders who were Jews and who had invested "a large amount of capital" in the enterprise. The directors' answer to Stuyvesant was a firm "no," which forced the governor to revoke a resolution that was about to go into effect ordering the New Amsterdam Jews "to depart at once."

From then on, for the nine additional years Stuyvesant ran New Netherland, he consoled himself by harassing the Jews with offensive restrictions—they could not hold public office, or run "open retail shops," so that livestock slaughtering became a Jewish trade. They were not allowed to join the militia and were compelled to pay a monthly exemption tax for not belonging. But they were allowed to own real estate, and to engage in trade, by specific order of the Company; and although they could not build a synagogue until 1695 that did not prevent them from forming Congregation Shearith Israel, now the oldest in North America.

With an even-handedness no one could confuse with justice, Stuyvesant also tormented the Quakers who were given shelter by the settlers in what is now Flushing, Queens, although the town's charter, dated 1645, promised its residents "liberty of conscience." He deported some Quakers to Rhode Island and arrested several others—including a leading citizen of the town and a leader in the Society of Friends, John Bowne, for letting the Quakers meet in his house. That united the community in a formal protest, the famous "Flushing Remonstrance," signed by thirty-one men, Quakers and non-Quakers together.

Stuyvesant's reaction was to get tougher than before. He arrested the Flushing sheriff and the town clerk and suspended two justices of the peace. He banished John Bowne to Holland. Bowne told the Company what was happening, and the Company told Stuyvesant to stop in a graceful but firm letter:

although we heartily desire that these and other sectarians remained away from there, yet as they do not, we doubt very much, whether we can proceed against them rigorously without diminishing the population and stopping immigration, which must be favored at a so tender stage of the country's existence. You may therefore shut your eyes, at least not force people's consciences, but allow every one to have his own belief, as long as he behaves quietly and legally, gives no offence to his neighbors and does not oppose the government.[2]

Long before the English took over, the West India Company had reconciled itself to disappointing New Netherland profits. (If the yields had been greater, Stuyvesant might have had the money to prepare a better defense.) No matter. New Amsterdam, the farms and farm villages on Manhattan Island and around it, and the settlements in the Hudson River valley, such as they were, had acquired a character not at all like that of the other North American colonies. The difference was New Netherland's national and religious diversity, which Stuyvesant saw as a drawback. In 1661, he wrote the Company:

the English and French colonies are continued and populated by their own nation and countrymen and consequently bound together more firmly and united, while your Honors' colonies in New-Netherland are only gradually and slowly peopled by the scrapings of all sorts of nationalities (few excepted), who consequently have the least interest in the welfare and maintenance of the commonwealth.[3]

Stuyvesant's immediate concern, on that occasion, was the arrival of French Huguenots in the vicinity of what is now New Paltz in Ulster County. His general perception was accurate, and he can hardly be blamed for his failure to anticipate the advantages that would accrue to diversity long after their Honors had any proprietary interest in the outcome.

2. Quoted in Michael Kammen, *Colonial New York: A History* (New York: Cha[ ] Scribner's Sons, 1975), p. 62.
3. Quoted in *ibid.*, p. 63.

Deborah Moody, settled with a group of dissenters near Gravesend Bay, now the Bensonhurst section of Brooklyn.

The autocratic Stuyvesant, who governed New Netherland for
the last seventeen of the forty years of Dutch control, did his
mean-spirited best to subvert the Company's tolerant policy.
Stuyvesant, the son of a minister and a soldier by profession,
was prejudiced against almost anyone who did not belong to the
Dutch Reformed Church; his special antipathies were toward
Jews, Quakers, and Lutherans. When he arrived to take command, New Amsterdam was disorderly, even for a seaport.
Stuyvesant imagined that he could run it like a military garrison,
with a strong emphasis on discipline. He favored religious conformity if mostly for the sake of orderliness.

The Company, on the other hand, wanted more settlers. Its
permissiveness, while right in step with Holland's viewpoint at
the time, was commercial rather than theological. If a settler
could be found, the Company directors did not want him disqualified on religious grounds. If a tolerant attitude attracted pioneers, well and good. The first Jews arrived in 1654—a few
from Holland first, and then a group of twenty-three, mostly
Spanish or Portuguese originally, who had fled to Holland from
their native lands and had then been sent to Brazil as West India
Company colonists. They had been driven out of Brazil by the
Portuguese, who took over from the Dutch. The twenty-three
took it for granted that they would be welcome in the West
India Company's New Amsterdam. On the contrary, as soon as
Stuyvesant understood that they meant to settle there he wrote
an immoderate letter asking the Company to recall them and to
stop sending Jews to New Netherland altogether. Stuyvesant's
minister, Johannes Megapolensis, who had served first up the
Hudson at Rensselaerswyck, seconded Stuyvesant's complaint:
"We have here Papists, Mennonites and Lutherans among the
Dutch, also many Puritans or Independents and many atheists
and various other servants of Baäl . . . it would create still
greater confusion, if the obstinate and immovable Jews came to
settle here."[1]

---

1. Quoted in Henri and Barbara Van der Zee, *A Sweet and Alien Land* (New York: Viking Press, 1978), p. 291.

The Company was completely out of sympathy with the Stuyvesant–Megapolensis argument. Its directors were convinced that Jewish settlers could help New Netherland as they had helped the United Netherlands since 1605, when the Jews had been allowed to establish their first congregation in Amsterdam. Moreover, the Company did not intend to insult the small but valued number—perhaps 4 percent—of shareholders who were Jews and who had invested "a large amount of capital" in the enterprise. The directors' answer to Stuyvesant was a firm "no," which forced the governor to revoke a resolution that was about to go into effect ordering the New Amsterdam Jews "to depart at once."

From then on, for the nine additional years Stuyvesant ran New Netherland, he consoled himself by harassing the Jews with offensive restrictions—they could not hold public office, or run "open retail shops," so that livestock slaughtering became a Jewish trade. They were not allowed to join the militia and were compelled to pay a monthly exemption tax for not belonging. But they were allowed to own real estate, and to engage in trade, by specific order of the Company; and although they could not build a synagogue until 1695 that did not prevent them from forming Congregation Shearith Israel, now the oldest in North America.

With an even-handedness no one could confuse with justice, Stuyvesant also tormented the Quakers who were given shelter by the settlers in what is now Flushing, Queens, although the town's charter, dated 1645, promised its residents "liberty of conscience." He deported some Quakers to Rhode Island and arrested several others—including a leading citizen of the town and a leader in the Society of Friends, John Bowne, for letting the Quakers meet in his house. That united the community in a formal protest, the famous "Flushing Remonstrance," signed by thirty-one men, Quakers and non-Quakers together.

Stuyvesant's reaction was to get tougher than before. He arrested the Flushing sheriff and the town clerk and suspended two justices of the peace. He banished John Bowne to Holland. Bowne told the Company what was happening, and the Company told Stuyvesant to stop in a graceful but firm letter:

although we heartily desire that these and other sectarians remained away from there, yet as they do not, we doubt very much, whether we can proceed against them rigorously without diminishing the population and stopping immigration, which must be favored at a so tender stage of the country's existence. You may therefore shut your eyes, at least not force people's consciences, but allow every one to have his own belief, as long as he behaves quietly and legally, gives no offence to his neighbors and does not oppose the government.[2]

Long before the English took over, the West India Company had reconciled itself to disappointing New Netherland profits. (If the yields had been greater, Stuyvesant might have had the money to prepare a better defense.) No matter. New Amsterdam, the farms and farm villages on Manhattan Island and around it, and the settlements in the Hudson River valley, such as they were, had acquired a character not at all like that of the other North American colonies. The difference was New Netherland's national and religious diversity, which Stuyvesant saw as a drawback. In 1661, he wrote the Company:

the English and French colonies are continued and populated by their own nation and countrymen and consequently bound together more firmly and united, while your Honors' colonies in New-Netherland are only gradually and slowly peopled by the scrapings of all sorts of nationalities (few excepted), who consequently have the least interest in the welfare and maintenance of the commonwealth.[3]

Stuyvesant's immediate concern, on that occasion, was the arrival of French Huguenots in the vicinity of what is now New Paltz in Ulster County. His general perception was accurate, and he can hardly be blamed for his failure to anticipate the advantages that would accrue to diversity long after their Honors had any proprietary interest in the outcome.

2. Quoted in Michael Kammen, *Colonial New York: A History* (New York: Charles Scribner's Sons, 1975), p. 62.
3. Quoted in *ibid.*, p. 63.

3

An English Province

*F*OR all its diversity, the colony was unmistakably Dutch in 1664. The striking exception was the eastern end of Long Island: towns like Southampton, East Hampton, and Southold, which had first been settled by Puritans from Connecticut in 1640, were clearly English. In forty years the population had grown to perhaps 9,000, New York City—the settlement at the southern tip of Manhattan Island, that is—to about 1,500. There were farms throughout what are today the other four boroughs of the city, in the present-day suburbs, and up both sides of the Hudson River valley. About three hundred people lived in the town of Albany (as Beverwyck, formerly Fort Orange, had been named).

The rate of population growth had been increasing because the Dutch, who were forever changing the rules, had made the requirements for a patroonship less ambitious and had reduced the size of the land grants accordingly. In 1629, a qualified entrepreneur who brought at least fifty tenant-farmers to New Netherland at his own expense had been awarded a vast tract of land for their settlement. He had been able to choose between eighteen miles of Hudson River waterfront property on one side and nine miles along both sides, with no limit on how far the boundaries might extend east or west. But fifty willing tenants fifteen years old or older had not been easy to find and the total expense of, in effect, establishing a sub-colony within the colony was great. On those terms, only a few investors had taken advantage of the patroon offer, and several of them, disenchanted, had soon returned their land to the Company. One great exception was Kileaen van Rensselaer, one of the Company's founder-members, whose enormous estate, Rensselaerswyck, eventually added up to a total of 700,000 acres in what are now Albany, Rensselaer, and Columbia counties. The Company did better with more modest terms after 1640: a grant of two hundred acres to the patroon who brought five settlers with him.

The size of the New York population was nothing to be ashamed of, but the Dutch record could not compare with the colonizing successes the English had had in Virginia, which had grown to 40,000, and in New England, which boasted about 50,000 residents. New Yorkers hoped that the province would do better under the English. The change from the West India Company's property to the Duke of York's proprietary was anything but dramatic. Like the Company's directors, the duke was interested in New York's money-making possibilities. But since New York's return on all the investments that had been made in it was low, and no one had a brilliant scheme for increasing its yield, the duke's expectations were limited.

The New Yorkers wanted more foreign trade and more political freedom, and some of them expected that under the English they would get more of both They were disappointed. The first English governor, Richard Nicholls, who had commanded the four-ship attack that had captured New Amsterdam, received an unctuous welcoming letter from the City's *burgomasters* and *schepens*. They offered him obedience and predicted that under his administration New York would "bloom and grow like the Cedars of Lebanon." Nicholls's regime lasted only four years—by the third he was pleading to be relieved of his assignment—and of blooming and growing there was precious little. He was replaced in 1668 by Francis Lovelace, and in the course of the next one hundred years the governorship changed hands twenty-four more times (including Captain Anthony Colve's six-month term in 1673–74 when the Dutch were back in control for a brief reprise).

Some of the British governors were fairly capable: Sir Edmund Andros (1674–1682), who replaced Colve, Thomas Dongan (1686–1691), and Robert Hunter (1720–1728); and some were quite good on their own terms, like Richard Coote, Earl of Bellomont (1698–1701), and William Tryon (1771–1778), the next to last on the list. Others were pathetic, like Sir Danvers Osborn (1753), who committed suicide six days after he had taken office, or peculiar, like Edward Hyde, Viscount Cornbury (1702–1708), who liked to patrol the ramparts of the fort dressed like his cousin, Queen Anne. The governorship almost always went to someone to whom the Crown owed a favor. The salary was modest, but it was understood that the governor was free to make as much money as he could on his own account as long as the royal treasury also showed a profit.

New York gradually turned English. English colonists arrived, but not with a rush. London did not dream of outlawing the Dutch language or of tampering with the Dutch flavor of local customs, and Dutch Calvinism maintained its prominent place for quite a long time. But another side to the relaxed English attitude was failure to respond to New York's deep desire for a measure of home rule. The children and then the grandchildren of settlers began to take places in New York affairs. The leading New York families—Van Cortlandts, Bayards, Van Rensselaers, Stuyvesants, Livingstons, Beekmans, and Morrises among them—were at least as disappointed as the Crown by the sluggish rate of the province's growth. They also believed, with varying degrees of conviction, that the more enterprising of the colonists—themselves, to be precise—should have a larger share in deciding how New York should be governed.

Governor Nicholls wrote a new legal code for New York, trying to resolve some of the infinite confusions between the Dutch and the English ways of settling disputes. He also appointed a provincial secretary and a four-man council of prominent New Yorkers. But Nicholls did not provide an elected assembly, which was what New York wanted, or even town meetings like those in New England. All the power that mattered remained in the governor's hands. Nicholls's legal code was not much help, for that matter. No one really understood New York law until 1752, when a pair of New Yorkers, William Smith, Jr., and William Livingston, wrote a new code. Governor Andros recommended that New York should have an assembly to be elected by all the freeholders in the province, but London thought that was unnecessary. Governor Dongan went right ahead and established just such an assembly without asking for permission. When London heard what Dongan had done, the assembly was abolished.

Business did grow, but slowly. Direct dealing with the Netherlands was stopped, and the increase in trade with England was much less than the New York merchants had anticipated. New York sold wheat to Boston and furs to Europe. New York imported rum and molasses from the West Indies, wines from Madeira, and "Indian goods"—blankets, woolens, guns, gunpowder, and lead, the commodities the Indians wanted in exchange for their furs—from Europe.

After 1678, New York City had a formal monopoly on export trade in addition to a monopoly on the carrying trade on the Hudson between New York and Albany. Albany was greatly dissatisfied with the arrangement. New York City was also designated the sole port of entry to the province, to the particular outrage of the port of Southampton, Long Island. New York City was given a monopoly on processing flour for export, irritating a score of flour-processors and would-be processors in the province's other towns. In not much more than a twinkling, English policy had set in motion the upstate–downstate rivalry that has been repeated, on one issue after another, ever since.

In 1685, the Duke of York became James II, King of England, and New York became a "Crown colony." The following year Albany received a charter that gave *it* a monopoly over fur-trading with the Indians. Albany felt a little better about the collection of special privileges New York City had acquired, although Albany fur traders deeply resented the fact that their cargoes had to be reshipped for Europe from the port of New York. But Schenectady's fur traders, who had been Albany's main competitors in the trade with the Indians, could not have been more unhappy.

King James dismayed almost all New Yorkers by deciding to combine New York, New Jersey, and all the New England colonies into one large dominion called "New England," with New York's former governor Andros as governor of the whole and with Boston as his headquarters. The plan implied that any hope for self-rule for New York was doomed. Boston, which liked the scheme as little as New York, rebelled against it and put Andros in jail.

New York soon followed Boston's lead. On May 31, 1689, the militia officers on duty at Fort James—six captains, of whom the senior was a well-to-do importer, Jacob Leisler—stopped taking their orders from Lieutenant Governor Francis Nicholson, who was running the colony's affairs with a three-man Council of New York's wealthiest citizens, Frederick Philipse (probably *the* wealthiest), Nicholas Bayard, and Stephen Van Cortlandt. Henceforth, the captains announced, the fort would belong to the revolution they were leading. Not long afterward, Captain Leisler and his supporters called a convention of delegates from all of New York's twelve counties, and nine of them responded. The convention in turn appointed a ten-man Committee of Safety, with Leisler as "Commander of the Province" empowered to act with full authority in all matters legal, administrative, and military. Nicholson wisely decided to leave New York and go to England in order to file a complaint.

Commander Leisler and his fellow rebels were not so much anti-English as anti-Catholic. They were convinced that Catholic King James meant to force the Dominion of New England, including New York, into Catholicism. But as so often happened during the seventeenth and eighteenth centuries, the news from abroad was far out of date: James had abandoned his throne six months before the New York rebellion and had fled to France to take refuge at the court of Louis XIV. His Protestant son-in-law, William III of Holland, and James's Protestant daughter, Mary, had become king and queen of England.

Nevertheless, the rebellion was an accomplished fact; Leisler and his associates, who were mostly Dutch, ran the colony until March 1691. They established an elected New York Assembly—or reestablished it, counting Governor Dongan's experiment as the first. The Assembly passed some laws, and New York City was permitted to elect its mayor. No one could deny, when the English reappeared to assert control, that New York had maintained a reasonably orderly functioning government.

But Leisler's rebellion, as it came to be called, was far from successful. As commander, Leisler became almost as arbitrary as the Dutch and English governors had been, and he filled the jails with his critics. Though he was well-to-do, he frightened the very rich: the big landowners, the most successful merchants, the lawyers. In the beginning, he had wanted to break away from England, and naturally the Crown officials feared him on that account. His supporters were not the poor but successful shopkeepers, small businessmen, tavern-owners, skilled laborers, and craftsmen. New York was split into two factions, Leislerian and anti-Lieslerian parties that continued to oppose each other long after the rebellion had ended and long after Leisler was dead.

By the end of his twenty months in power, all Leisler wanted for himself was recognition by William and Mary that his intentions had been good. William had no thought of going on with the idea of a Dominion of New England, and in January 1690 he had appointed a new governor for New York, Henry Sloughter. It took Sloughter a year and two months, until March 19, 1691, to get to New York City. Meanwhile the new lieutenant governor, Richard Ingoldsby, arrived unannounced, and without papers to prove his authority. (Sloughter had them.) Leisler did not know whether he should surrender the fort as Ingoldsby demanded, urged on by Philipse, Bayard, and Van Cortlandt. Leisler and Ingoldsby began to argue. In a fight that followed, Leisler's men killed some of Ingoldsby's soldiers.

When Governor Sloughter finally arrived, New York City was virtually in a civil war. Leisler still held the fort. When Sloughter demanded its surrender, Leisler waited a fatal twenty-four hours before he handed it over. Sloughter had Leisler and his aide, his son-in-law Jacob Milborne, and a group of their cohorts arrested for treason. A trial was held. Leisler and Milborne were hanged and beheaded—excessive punishment, for certain—and six of the others were sentenced to death. (Their

sentences were later commuted, and they were all released.)
New Yorkers in general, including many of Leisler's political
adversaries, thought the charge and the punishment were unjust.
So many people wrote to England in protest that Parliament
reviewed the case a little less than four years later and reversed
the verdict. Leisler's and Milborne's names were cleared, and
their estates were restored to their families.

The two factions that had evolved during the twenty months
continued for a long time. The colony was back under the
Crown's control, but the elected Assembly continued and the
Governor's Council developed into something like the upper
house of a legislature. The Leisler party, representing artisans,
shopkeepers, and farmers, continued to exist in opposition to
the Philipse faction, the rich merchants and land barons. In
1695, the Leislerians won control of the Assembly and, among
other acts, repealed New York City's flour-processing monopoly. All the way down to the Revolution, the ghosts of the
Leisler rebellion were in evidence. Lewis Morris won over the
old Leislerians, and the De Lanceys and the Livingstons took
command of the Philipse faction until the two family alliances
split and became arch-rivals.

4

Prelude to Separation

*C*ONSIDERING the diffident, exploitive, and neglectful attitudes the Dutch and English colonizers had demonstrated, it was a wonder that a colony of some stature called New York existed at the end of its first hundred years. New York still lagged behind the other English colonies in almost every measure, but it was gathering energy for a period of expansion in all sorts of activity.

The occasional colonist with a choice of where to go had been likely to pass New York by in favor of Virginia or New England; but some of the peculiarities that had seemed unattractive in the seventeenth century were proving to be New York's assets. The population's diversity in national background and religious preference seemed directly related to the diversity of ways in which New Yorkers were learning to make money. The colony's concern about self-rule, which had produced a degree of untidiness in public affairs, was connected with a degree of concern for the common good. Admittedly, the one time all of New York remembered clearly that upstate and downstate, including Long Island, belonged together was when England or New England or the French did something that New York disliked.

The governor in 1724 was William Burnet, polite, scholarly son of an Anglican bishop. Indian affairs were much on Burnet's mind, as was France's plan to outflank the British colo-

29

nies, confining them to the Atlantic coast by building a chain of forts from eastern Canada westward and down the Mississippi to Louisiana. Those two subjects interlocked because the Indians in the northern and western parts of what is now New York held a balance of power in the competition between England and France; they were the hunters who supplied the beaver and deer skins.

Burnet's idea was to bid for the furs of the western or "far" Indians by building a trading post at Oswego on the eastern shore of Lake Ontario. It would be fairly accessible to all the members of the Iroquois League of Six Nations—the Senecas, Cayugas, Onondagas, Oneidas, Mohawks, and Tuscaroras (the last newly arrived from the Carolinas). In addition, Burnet persuaded the New York Assembly to prohibit Albany's sprightly trade in Indian goods with the French in Montreal. By depriving the French of trading materials, Burnet calculated, New York could induce the western Indians to forget Montreal and to deliver their pelts to Oswego and thence to Albany instead.

Burnet's logic was excellent. But the Albany merchants hated to stop selling Indian goods to the French; and the New York City merchants, including the influential James De Lancey, hated to stop importing Indian goods from England to sell to Albany. The trading ban, moreover, was well nigh unenforceable. Burnet had to settle for a drastic modification of his scheme. Still, the new trading post, Fort Oswego, remained in being. As the years went by, the quantity of furs reaching Albany increased, and in a few years Oswego replaced Albany as the center for fur trading.

By the time of the Revolution, fifty years later, New York's population had grown from 40,000 to 175,000, not counting the Algonquins and the Iroquois. New York City and Albany—the port and the trading center—grew fastest, but they remained small towns. New York City's built-up area, which contained about 20,000 residents, was nearly all below what is now Chambers Street, the northern boundary of City Hall Park. The southern tip of Manhattan Island was not nearly so large as it is today because the waterfront filling-in process, which is still going on, had hardly begun. Albany was about one-seventh as big as New York City, with a population approaching 3,000. In short, nearly everybody in New York lived in the country, and close to the water—whether the water was a lake, the Atlantic Ocean, Long Island Sound, the Bay, or the Hudson River.

About one-half of the colony's population were English, including transplants from New England, Connecticut, and Rhode Island. About one-eighth, or 22,000, were Dutch, and the Dutch still dominated Albany. But that left perhaps 75,000 New Yorkers who were neither Dutch nor English. While everybody used Dutch words like *waffle, cruller, cookie, coleslaw,* and *yacht,* and many were fond of doughnuts, ice-skating, and Santa Claus, and while the new houses on Broadway and Broad Street in New York City were the duplicates of the new houses being built in London, just as the latest fashions in ladies' and gentlemen's dress were English, a number of the other European national cultures were represented in New York, including French, German, Scots, Irish, and Swedish. The French Huguenot families, settled in communities like New Paltz, had contributed powerful leaders like the De Lanceys, the DePeysters, and the Jays. Palatine Germans had founded Newburgh and also settled west of Albany along the Schoharie and Mohawk rivers.

There were at least 20,000 blacks, some in every county but most of them near the mouth of the Hudson and about 5,000 in New York City itself. The great majority of the blacks had been imported from the West Indies, not from Africa. Slavery and the indenture system, by which a colonist agreed to trade off a specific number of years of his labor—usually five—in return for his passage and a start on a life in the New World, were built into New York's economic system. Slavery had been part of the West India Company's plan. Farming and nearly every other kind of New York enterprise leaned heavily on labor that was not paid adequately, or not paid at all. The well-to-do in New York City could not have maintained their large, handsome brick houses without a number of slave house servants. (There was no heat except fireplaces, and no plumbing, and no sewer system. All waste material was carried to the nearest river and dumped into it, usually at night.)

The principal activity of New Yorkers was farming, and the

principal crops were wheat and corn. The fur trade—the only trade that had interested the Dutch investors—was dwindling as the best hunting grounds moved west and north. Forest products—lumber, tar, pitch, turpentine, and tall masts for ships—had begun to grow in importance. Yet New York lacked a suitable staple for export—something comparable, for instance, to Virginia's tobacco. New York did its best to substitute a variety of commodities: beeswax, pork, bacon, barrel staves, candles, hardtack, chocolate, flax, hemp, potash and pearl ash. London and Bristol were New York's main markets, along with the other colonies and the British islands in the West Indies.

The great trouble was that England cared little for most of what New York had to export, except for furs, flaxseed, and iron. New York's balance of trade with England was absurdly unfavorable, and the colony was thus drained of the hard money England demanded for its manufactures. As a result, trade with the West Indies was most attractive—especially with those islands that could pay with gold or silver or by exchanging commodities that the English did want, like sugar, cotton, spices, and logs. Jamaica was therefore New York's main market in the West Indies, with Curaçao and Honduras not far behind. New York exporters also bought considerable quantities of New England fish and South Carolina rice, which they added to their cargoes of New York flour for shipment to Spain and Portugal.

Those New Yorkers who neither farmed nor traded for furs nor imported and exported goods and commodities were engaged in a wide variety of other occupations. Sugar refineries had been built, and brewing and distilling were also highly profitable—they used up grains that were grown locally and turned them into liquid products that were comparatively easy to transport. New York, and New York City especially, seemed to have an unquenchable thirst. It was said about Boston that a man could buy a drink in every eighth building in town; in New York City no one needed to walk nearly that far. The place bristled with bars, inns, taverns, and grogshops. While the rich preferred imported Madeira, the wine from the islands off Morocco, to any other beverage, it was usually too expensive for ordinary drinking. (Richard and Theophylact Bache, wine merchants who specialized in Madeira, had become extremely wealthy.) But New Yorkers were also fond of claret, burgundy, sack, port, champagne, brandy, beer, porter, West Indian rum, New York rum, New England rum, and a variety of home brews that were distinguished by little except their alcoholic content. New Yorkers drank in their leisure time, and they also drank whenever hard physical labor was called for, like digging a ditch or raising a roof. Manhattan Island was dotted with orchards, but the fruit was good for only one purpose: to make wine, brandy, cider, or a fruit punch to disguise the taste of home brew.

A small but first-class shipbuilding business was developing, with one large shipyard on the East River. Several iron furnaces were in operation, notably the Ancram Works on Livingston Manor and the Stirling Ironworks in Orange County. A considerable amount of whaling was done, and such related activities as making containers for whale oil had developed into a sizable industry. The whaling port of Sag Harbor, on Long Island, which had not been settled until 1712, had boomed right past East Hampton and Southampton—in terms of port traffic, at any rate.

Lumbering was developing from solely a necessity of life into a trade of considerable value. Almost all of New York's 47,687 square miles were originally forest-covered, with vast stands of white pine in the Adirondacks and Catskills and hardwoods—cleared off early because the land where they grew was suitable for agriculture—to the west. The first sawmill in New Netherland was established in about 1623; ships' masts were constructed from upper Hudson valley timber by 1699. Log drives from the upper Hudson and the Schroon to Glens Falls were among the earliest in the country. In 1763 Quaker Abraham Wing built a sawmill at the falls, and a settlement grew up around this and other, smaller mills in the immediate area. Within a century the Hudson valley would be the heart of the lumber industry in America.

In the towns, especially Albany and New York City, craftsmen and artisans were making a variety of things for sale to their neighbors. There were, among many others, cordwainers (shoemakers), joiners, coopers, barbers, wigmakers, blacksmiths, carpenters, bakers, victualers, butchers, carters, tailors, weavers, felt-makers, hatters, goldsmiths, silversmiths, pot makers, sailmakers, pewterers, saddlers, wheelwrights, and confectioners. There were printers, newspaper publishers, booksellers, and a busy trade after 1754 in inkpots, ink bottles, and inkstands. There were schoolteachers, librarians, doctors, surgeons, and a profusion of lawyers.

Though the subject was not much discussed in public. a good deal of New York's cash income came from piracy, or "privateering" as it was called whenever England was at war and it became licensed and perfectly legal (provided the privateers confined their captures to the ships and cargoes of England's enemies, and no others). Some of New York's best families were heavily invested in privateering, and Crown officers, including New York governors, often shared in the loot. A New York shipowner, or a group of New York businessmen who had chartered a ship, armed the vessel with a few guns. They hired a captain and a crew and applied through the governor for a privateer's commission from the king of England. It was a high-risk gamble, for there was always the danger that, instead of taking, a privateer might be taken. But the rewards could be high, and the owners or investors, the captain, and the crew of the privateer were entitled to divide up what they captured on the high seas according to a prearranged agreement on shares. A New York court approved each such agreement, and if disputes arose afterwards, as they usually did, the court settled the claims.

New York privateers had many legal prizes to hunt for, since England was constantly at war with one country or another, but the ocean seas are wide and the temptation to take a neutral nation's ship, or even a friendly ship, was considerable. That, of course, became piracy, not privateering, and was as unlawful as taking any ship during the occasional years when England was at peace. New York pirates had an effective gambit for bringing illegal seizures back to the port of New York. They took their prizes to some remote island like Madagascar, in the Indian Ocean off the east coast of Africa, where they transferred the stolen cargoes to innocent-looking, unarmed New York merchant ships. At New York it was difficult to distinguish between legal imports and stolen goods accompanied by faked papers.

Captain William Kidd of Sloat Lane (now Beaver Street), New York City, stood as the prototype of the successful privateer turned pirate. Some modern historians argue that Kidd was a victim rather than a criminal; that he had been talked into piracy by his eminent backers, including Governor Bellomont, Robert Livingston, King William, and five of the highest lords of the realm—all of whom insisted that they wanted Kidd to catch pirates, not to become one. The captain's story was that his crew had mutinied and forced him to turn pirate. He turned himself in at Boston, where he was arrested, taken to London, tried, and executed in May, 1701.

But Captain Kidd's dismal end did not dampen New York's enthusiasm for privateering, which rose to a peak during the French and Indian War (1755–1763). New York merchants, glowing with speculative fever, put at least thirty-four privateers into action, feeling that the oceans were paved with gold. In 1744, four of them—the *Royal Hester,* the *Polly,* the *Clinton,* and the *Mary Anne*—representing a combined investment of perhaps £10,000, travelled as a four-ship navy with an agreement among themselves to share spoils. Off Grand Caicos Island, north of Haiti, the New Yorkers came upon seven French ships sailing as a fleet and captured six of them. The total prize to be divided was an estimated £22,000, and law suits over its distribution dragged on for years. The ordinary seaman's share in "The Great Capture," as the New Yorkers called their victory, was extraordinarily large. It worked out at £25 per man for the smallest crewman-shareholder, whereas a green crew member, with luck, might expect perhaps a £3 share of an average prize.

Speculators with money left over after they had invested in privateering ventures, or with profits from privateering, were absorbed by the possibilities of the fortunes that could be made in real estate. Successful merchants owned their homes and stores to begin with and went on as quickly as they could to add wharves and then country estates within easy sailing distance of their places of business. Next they gambled on backcountry acreage on the theory that, in the long run, the growing population would have to have room to expand.

There were no banks in a modern sense, and the British government had banned the issue of paper money by New York and all the other colonies in 1764. The shortage of currency in New York was a constant annoyance. The mere mechanics of a financial transaction of any size could be absurdly complicated. In rural communities, barter was the everyday system for exchanging goods and services; and in the cities and towns it was not surprising for a retail merchant to advertise his willingness to accept "country pay"—meaning that he was willing to make a swap. A rich New Yorker with currency, bills of exchange, or bills of credit that were acceptable in London was likely to gamble (like modern banks) by making personal loans called "bonds" or "notes" to those he regarded as likely to repay the principal with interest. He could purchase a share in almost any venture and then perhaps sell it within the hour. Or he could write marine insurance. If those risks seemed insufficient, he could buy New York City lottery tickets. The odds were outrageous, but the lotteries raised money for worthy projects like building a college or a new jail, repairing City Hall, or supplying New York hemp-growers with a subsidy.

Not many New York merchants were wealthy enough, or daring enough, to engage in every last one of these speculations. In 1775 a group of one hundred formed the New York Chamber of Commerce, and its membership included all but a few of the men who could qualify. However, New York's commercial leaders had emerged as a powerful segment of society, taking much of the initiative in running the colony's affairs away from the aristocracy of the landowners, both Dutch and English. Many of them, furthermore, were allied with that aristocracy as sons and grandsons and sons-in-law. While it looked as if their risky enterprises were mere gambles, the consistent winners among the New York merchants felt that they were, on the contrary, investing in good judgment and superior information about the ways of the eighteenth-century world. Indeed, for mere colonials, they were generally sophisticated students of world affairs, making money much of the time by anticipating markets and prices and maneuvering to be able to sell what was wanted at the right time for the highest price.

Their philosophy—to the limited extent that they were guided by philosophy—was founded on marketplace values. They assumed that man was by nature first and foremost acquisitive. They were assertive in their competition with each other and the businessmen in every other land, and they were convinced that the proper goal of public policy was to help those who were helping commerce expand. To be sure, they were outnumbered in New York by farmers, yeomen, artisans, and craftsmen by a ratio of perhaps 1,500 to 1, but the population in general shared many of the wealthy merchants' views: man was potentially good and capable of unlimited improvement. A modest government, with circumscribed powers, seemed in accord with those fundamentals. The more they experienced rule from the far side of the Atlantic, the greater their devotion to home rule grew.

King George II died in 1760, and his plump, stubborn, twenty-two-year-old grandson became King George III. New York, the most English of the American colonies, had led the step-by-step movement toward separation. New York was the headquarters for the English Army in America; the terrain between Albany and Fort Ticonderoga was the critical focus of the French and Indian War; and after the war was concluded in 1763—the English won a great and stunningly expensive victory—New York balked at the young king's attempts to get the colonies to pay some of the cost of their defense. Quite apart from the debt the British had already run up, it looked as if a British army of perhaps as many as ten thousand men might be needed in America to protect the colonies against the Indians.

Prime Minister Lord George Grenville imagined that the colonists might not mind paying the old taxes on imports, including molasses and several other West Indies products, which had been in existence for some time but had never been collected in an efficient manner. That notion was incorrect, and his effort failed. The next money-raising scheme was to sell the colonists blue paper tax stamps, costing from twopence to ten pounds apiece, and require that one of them be affixed to every newspaper and legal document, along with decks of playing cards, pairs of dice, and a long list of other items. New Yorkers were also supposed to surrender a tax stamp wherever they bought a drink in a tavern, an annoyance that they found intolerable.

New York was first among the colonies to petition the king and Parliament to drop the stamp tax, which was even more odious than the import taxes because it had nothing to do with trade regulation. It was an excise tax, pure and simple, designed to raise money for the Crown and, as dozens of New York lawyers were ready to attest, entirely illegal and beyond Parliament's tax power. The phraseology of the petition was so bold, unfortunately, that no M.P. was willing to introduce it. On the last day of October 1765, New York's merchants signed a nonimportation agreement: they agreed to boycott British goods until the Stamp Act was repealed. One week later Philadelphia's merchants followed suit, and so, after another month, did Boston's.

New York's newspapers, especially Hugh Gaine's *Mercury,* William Weyman's *Gazette,* and John Holt's *Weekly Journal,* seethed with righteous indignation against the stamp tax outrage—as well they might, considering they were high on the list of items to be stamped. "It is better to wear a homespun coat than to lose our liberty," the *Gazette* declared. A market for home manufactures, which were prohibited, was opened on Broad Street. New Yorkers who loved tea did their best to make do with an ersatz substitute of sassafras bark and sage. The New Yorkers formed a Committee of Correspondence to write to the protest leaders in the other colonies and exchange information about "the impending dangers." The law was scheduled to go into effect on November 1, and James McEvers, a New York City merchant, had been appointed to sell the stamps. After reading the papers and listening to the tenor of the conversations that were going on, McEvers concluded that he would prefer not to have the job and resigned on August 30.

From October 7 to October 25, New York City was host to an emergency meeting of delegates from nine of the thirteen colonies that was later called the Stamp Act Congress, and the Sons of Liberty, New York's most radical organization, made its first public appearances. The Sons of Liberty made no bones about believing that force—physical violence—was the way to bring the king, his ministers, and Parliament to their senses. They were mostly small shopkeepers, working men, and artisans, or "Mechanics" in the popular if somewhat fuzzy term they used to describe themselves. They represented a lot of muscle power, and they had several capable leaders. Among them were John Lamb, the son of a prosperous wine merchant, who went on to a distinguished career in the Continental Army; and Isaac Sears, a waterfront hero, the former captain of the privateer *Harlequin,* who at thirty-five was helping his father-in-law run the sailors' and boatmen's favorite alehouse, Jasper Drake's Tavern at the head of Beekman Slip.

The loathed stamps arrived on October 23 and were put ashore under cover of darkness and stored in Fort George. A week went by. Finally, on the night of October 31, the New York mob—the Liberty Boys, primarily, but with volunteer reinforcements—swarmed through the streets, filling property-owners with dread because the city was highly inflammable and there was no telling how far the enraged citizens might go. Actually, for all the noise they made, the Liberty Boys were restrained: they burned an effigy of Cadwallader Colden, the acting governor, along with his coach and sleigh; they ransacked the elegant home of the English commander of the New York garrison, Major Thomas James; they milled around the fort as if they were about to storm and take it, as they could have done with ease.

Colden, his Council, and General Thomas Gage (commanding all the British forces in America) were at least equally restrained. The soldiers did not fire. Colden handed the stamps over to city officials, who moved them to City Hall on Wall Street at the top of Broad Street, and the terror subsided. The stamps were kept under lock and key until March 1766, when Parliament repealed the offensive law.

New York rejoiced over the Stamp Act's repeal, not realizing that the king and his ministers were going to make similar mistakes, and worse ones, in the decade to come. Colden and Gage understood that civil war had been avoided by a narrow margin. They could not understand how completely the Stamp

Act furor foreshadowed the war for independence by teaching the colonies to act together politically in congress, and by forcing the American leaders to improvise a considerable part of the devices the Continental Congress would employ on a larger scale to sustain that long conflict.

5

An Odious Reputation

A new governor, William Tryon, arrived at New York in July 1771. He had been serving as the governor of North Carolina and was replacing John Murray, Earl of Dunmore, who had been transferred to the governorship of Virginia. Tryon, forty-six years old, brought his wife and daughter with him. He was an attractive, realistic career soldier with little or no interest in serving as a colonial governor; but in the imaginations of those New Yorkers who were most out of sympathy with the radical tactics and objects of the Sons of Liberty, he was a hero.

Two months earlier, on May 16, Tryon had used his small professional army to disperse a band of angry, leaderless, up-country North Carolina farmers who called themselves "Regulators" from a field on the bank of Alamance Creek, twenty miles west of Hillsboro, and on the following day he had had half a dozen of them hanged for treason. Quite a few New Yorkers hoped that the new governor would deal with the New York protesters in an equally forceful manner. Their hopes were based on misconceptions, starting with the assumption that the Regulators and the Liberty Boys were alike.

The Regulators had not been a part of the organized anti-British movement. While they were opposed to government authority, including royal authority, the specific object of their anger had been the Hillsboro county register, Edmund Fanning, Tryon's friend and protégé. The Regulators were convinced

Fanning had been charging them exorbitant official fees and pocketing the excess. Fanning was about as American as an American could be—the great-grandson of one Edmund Fanning who had settled at New London in 1653, a Yale graduate, Class of 1757, and a man who had made his home in Hillsboro long before Tryon had ever heard of the place. Furthermore, Tryon, the soldier, had done his best to *avoid* shooting at the Regulators. The North Carolinians had begun their campaign to make Fanning's life miserable by shooting at his house in the spring of 1768 and had gone on to whip him, drive him out of town, and burn down his handsome house before Tryon finally marched from New Bern to put a stop to their riots. Three years of hesitation in the face of the Regulators' provocations had been something less than a hair-trigger response.

Fanning, most wisely, had left North Carolina with Tryon and was acting as his secretary. Undoubtedly he helped the new governor understand the complexity of the province's politics. Tryon quickly made an excellent impression with nearly everyone in New York except the De Lanceys and their allies by telling the De Lanceys, in no uncertain terms, that he really intended to govern New York Province rather than to take orders from the De Lancey party or from the New York Assembly. The Livingston party, a coalition of upper Hudson River valley landlords and some of the merchants in Albany and New York, was particularly pleased by Tryon's challenge to the De Lancey–Philipse party because the Livingstons, with their allies, were the De Lanceys' main rivals for power within the province. The Livingstons had taken over control of the New York Assembly in 1761 and had kept it until 1768. Then, in 1769, the De Lanceys had made a surprising political comeback in the election by cooperating with the radicals, of all people—the members and friends of the Sons of Liberty.

Governor Tryon may have intended to be a real governor, but it was at least a quarter of a century too late for him to do so. For all their rivalries, regroupings, and realignments, the De Lanceys and the Livingstons were much closer to each other than they were to Tryon or any other royal governor. They were in accord with every other group that was active in provincial affairs on the fundamental issue, home rule. In that sense, there were no Tories in New York but only Whigs of varying intensities. The De Lancey party argued that the Assembly embodied all of the powers of government. The Livingston party, on the other hand, held that they were shared—the division was not perfectly clear—by the governor and the Assembly. But no party, and no more than a handful of individuals, asserted that the governor alone had all the authority to rule New York.

Tryon's declarations may have been *pro forma*—the good soldier obeying orders received from higher headquarters. Except for the magnificent local oysters, there was nothing about New York that he liked. His real ambition was a regimental command on the other side of the Atlantic or possibly an appointment as one of the king's military aides. At any rate, Tryon soon perceived that New York's leaders were infinitely more serious about home rule, and especially the matter of taxation, than London appeared able to understand. In April 1774, Tryon sailed for a visit to London. The trip was partly for his health; he was suffering from the eighteenth-century doctors' multi-purpose diagnosis, "the gout." It was also partly to try to explain to the king and his ministers that the American colonies—and New York in particular—were in no mood to temper their protests, which were focused that winter on the continuing tax on the East India Company's bargain-offer tea.

Tryon's ship had been gone only three weeks when New York City enacted its version of the "tea party" Boston had staged in December 1773. Two thousand indignant New Yorkers, organized by the Sons of Liberty, were down at The Battery waiting for the ships. The New York harbor pilots had been warned against going aboard to bring them into port. One of the ships' captains, who owned the eighteen cases of tea he had aboard, felt that he might be able to sneak his cargo ashore, but he was mistaken. Without bothering to disguise themselves as Indians, or anything else, the Sons of Liberty stormed aboard, found the cases, split them open, and dumped their contents into the East River.

The tea-tax question excited the political moderates, including a majority of the well-to-do men who were in the import-export business, as nothing had before. They were horrified by the king's tactic of appointing "consignees" to handle the tea sales in Boston, New York, Charleston, and Philadelphia: if the British could designate single-commodity monopolies to individual favorites, all the other merchants engaged in the same trade could be ruined. And they were appalled by the king's order that the port of Boston was to be shut down completely as of June 1 as punishment for having held its tea party. If Boston could be wiped out with the stroke of a pen, how long could New York expect to survive?

While their cautious counterparts in Boston were trying to make amends—a group of one hundred Boston merchants had offered to pay for the water-damaged tea, and Benjamin Franklin, among others, applauded the gesture—the New York moderates packed a Committee of Fifty-One with men of their own outlook, generally on the Livingston-party side of most issues. They wanted to stand with Boston. They wanted to call a Congress of deputies from all the colonies so that the rules for a boycott of British goods could be uniform and fully understood in every American port.

They picked Isaac Low, a wealthy merchant of a conservative temper, as the committee's chairman. The vice chairman was John Alsop, an importer whose specialty had been tea and whose political views were slightly more conservative than Low's. Among the other members were Philip Livingston, an importer; James Duane, who was married to Philip's niece; and the brilliant young lawyer John Jay, who was twenty-nine years old and the husband of Sarah Livingston, the youngest daughter of William Livingston. Before the summer was over, New York had named these leaders of the Committee of Fifty-One to represent New York—each colony was to have only one vote—at the first Continental Congress, along with four other moderates, William Floyd, Henry Wisner, John Haring, and Simon Boerum. On Virginia's suggestion, the Congress met in Carpenter's Hall in Philadelphia instead of in New York City.

The leading spirits on the Committee of Fifty-One had managed an extraordinary political coup. While the De Lancey party still dominated the New York Assembly, the Livingston party had made off with a glittering prize: effective control of New York's role in the first Congress and in the Continental Association, which the Congress created, and—by extension into 1775 and 1776—a major voice on the questions of war, independence, and statehood. The De Lanceys were outmaneuvered, and the Mechanics and the Sons of Liberty were for the time being eclipsed. Of the nine delegates, four were lawyers (Jay, Duane, Wisner, and William Livingston) and three were rich merchants (Philip Livingston, Alsop, and Low). Eight of the nine were from the southern part of the province, the exception being Wisner, from Orange County, northwest of New York City. Five of the nine were from New York City.

The conservative leanings of the New York delegation, and especially the prominence of Low and Alsop, confused the other colonies. Indeed, they have confused many of the historians who have written about it during the past two centuries. It has been fashionable to say that New York was "the most Tory" of the colonies—an almost perfectly meaningless generalization—because in April, May, June, and July of 1776 the New York delegates to the Second Continental Congress had an embarrassingly difficult time voting in favor of the Declaration of Independence.

In the fall of 1774, however, independence—or separation, as it was commonly called—was not an issue and, with rare exceptions, had not been discussed. The question that divided Americans was allegiance to the Continental Association that the Continental Congress established, and to the Continental Association's pledges against importing British goods or exporting to Great Britain until the Associators' grievances had been redressed. The New York delegates had next to no difficulty voting yea on all of that, and agreed that the Continental Congress would reconvene on May 10, 1775—if, by any chance, the king, Lord North, and Parliament had not set things right before then.

New York had played a leading role in the Stamp Act protest; it had enforced the 1770 non-importation agreements more stringently than had any other of the port cities; and now, as usual, it was a leader in the Continental Association's economic war, which was several degrees more rebellious than any of the earlier forms of retaliation. As a reward, the seriousness of New York's commitment was doubted by almost everyone, starting with all the other colonies and including Lieutenant Governor Cadwallader Colden, who was acting governor in Tryon's absence.

The Continental Association's non-import, non-export pledge differed in kind from, say, the 1770 non-importation protest because the Continental Congress had voted that it was to be enforced by local committees chosen locally, one for each county, city, and town. The merchants in the ports were not to import tea, to pick one example; but the Association was deciding, in addition, that no one was to drink tea, in case he should come upon a few pounds that had been smuggled into the colonies, except at the risk of harassment by his friends and neighbors, the members of his local committee.

The New York Assembly, which had already lost a considerable part of its legitimate authority to the Committee of Fifty-One, promptly squandered nearly all of the power it had left by refusing to accept the Continental Association altogether. The Assembly also decided against choosing a slate of New York delegates to the Second Continental Congress, should a second congress prove necessary. With those two negative votes, the Assembly wiped itself off the map in everything except a technical sense; it continued to meet for a time, but no one much cared how its votes went.

Since the Assembly would not act, the Committee of Fifty-One, enlarged to the Committee of Sixty by virtue of having added some of the Mechanics' favorite sons, did the job. It called for a new body, as the Continental Congress had suggested, to be called the New York Provincial Congress. The Provincial Congress then put forth a slate of delegates to the Second Continental Congress: Low, Alsop, Duane, Jay, Philip Livingston, and Henry Wisner were renominated, and George Clinton, Francis Lewis, Robert R. Livingston, Lewis Morris, and Philip Schuyler were added to the list. The delegates were even stronger and more determinedly anti-British than before. With that business out of the way, the Provincial Congress quickly emerged as New York's *de facto* government. It was not only the Continental Association's enforcer, but the province's legislature and executive authority, too; and, as the months went by and this improvised, upstart organization demonstrated a remarkable ability to accomplish what needed doing, it steadily gained support from the counties up the Hudson.

Still, New York's intentions were suspect. Reasonable men from Georgia to Massachusetts thought that if the Continental Association's non-import, non-export rules were broken, New York was likely to be the first to break the agreement. As the protest movement changed over from economic sanctions to war, there were those who expected that New York would fail to do its part of the fighting. Unfair though these suspicions were, on occasion New York seemed bent on looking as if they were justified. There were many men in New York who were, and would remain, loyal to Great Britain and the king; and there were loyalists in all the other colonies, too. New York was the stronghold for the Church of England; from the moment the lines between the Associators and the non-Associators were drawn, men like the Reverend Myles Cooper, president of King's College, Dr. Charles Inglis, the acting rector of Trinity Parish, and above all Dr. Samuel Seabury of the West Chester Parish spoke and wrote with fervor on the loyalist side of the debate as it proceeded from point to point. Seabury, who often signed his essays "A West Chester Farmer," once remarked in a piece denouncing the Continental Association: "If I must be enslaved, let it be by a King, at least, and not by a parcel of upstart, lawless committeemen. If I must be devoured, let it be by the jaws of a lion, and not gnawed to death by rats and vermin."[1]

Impressive as the Anglican presence and the Anglican arguments may have been, they seemed to have no effect at all on the deliberations of the New York Provincial Congress. Since New York was the centerpiece of Great Britain's colonial adventures in North America—the key ground in her struggles

---

1. Quoted in Bruce Bliven, Jr., *Under the Guns: New York 1775–1776* (New York: Harper and Row, 1972), p. 53.

with France, her principal post office, the terminus of the trans-atlantic mail packet service from Falmouth, and the garrison town for the British army in North America whenever the soldiers' services were not required elsewhere—the British influence on New York had been unmistakable. (In happier days, New Yorkers had loved to watch the Redcoats march up Broadway from Fort George to the Commons and back whenever a holiday warranted a parade.) The province was full of office-holders whose incomes depended on the British government, and of Crown officials, judges, and customs agents many of whom were more nearly Englishmen on overseas assignment than Americans. If a substantial number of them had liked the Continental Association better than the king and Parliament, that would have been astonishing—even shocking.

After the war had begun, some of New York's detractors sounded as if they were quite unaware that the Committee of Sixty had won the contest in the preliminaries. A handbill that had originated in Philadelphia and was distributed throughout the colonies revealed the names of the six "most odious" Tories in New York—and, by implication, in America. The list included Cadwallader Colden and the Reverend Myles Cooper, who, odious or not, were undeniably out of sympathy with the Continental Association's policies. Then it named three New York merchants, John Watts, James De Lancey, and Henry White, who had been members of the Governor's Council and were well aware that they had lost the arguments. Watts and De Lancey, in despair, had abandoned their properties and sailed for England, and White was preparing to do so.

The sixth man, James Rivington, was a printer, a bookseller, and the editor-publisher of New York's liveliest and biggest weekly newspaper, the *Gazetteer,* with a circulation of about 3,500. Instead of great wealth, Rivington had debts: he had survived two bankruptcies but was headed for a third. The *Gazetteer*'s journalistic stock-in-trade, in addition to excellent foreign news, was political gossip, and Rivington had infuriated many of the most dedicated Associators by mean stories about their leaders, many of them in what was supposed to be humorous verse. (Rivington's favorite target was Isaac Sears, and the *Ga-*

zetteer invariably mentioned the fact that Sears had large, prominent ears.) Yet those who knew Rivington best insisted that he was not political and that he had no firm convictions about the Continental Association. They said that Rivington was simply trying to advance himself in New York society by printing what he thought its leaders would enjoy.

Rivington's friends may have been too tolerant. In April 1775, Rivington was named Royal Printer for New York; in 1777, with New York City in British hands, Rivington changed the name of his paper to the *Loyal Gazette* and then the *Royal Gazette* and made it the mouthpiece for the Loyalist point of view. To make the conundrum complete, in 1781 Rivington began sending secret information about the British to the Americans. After the British defeat, when George Washington had reentered New York City, Rivington stayed on. He removed the royal arms from his paper, changed its name to *Rivington's New York Gazette,* and continued to publish as if he assumed that all had been forgiven. He was mistaken. After about a month, a small committee headed by Isaac Sears, whose ears were still large and prominent, called on Rivington to talk things over. The *Gazette* never again appeared.

Much of the criticism that was directed against New York was no more significant than the "odious six" handbill, but on occasion New Yorkers seemed determined to help their detractors by appearing to be less than adamant in their devotion to the Glorious Cause. For example, on Sunday, June 25, 1775, New York endeavored to stage official welcomes for Washington, who had just been chosen commander in chief of the new Continental army, and its own Governor Tryon on his return from England. Washington was on his way from Philadelphia to Cambridge to take up his command, and was therefore merely passing through the city; Tryon, on the other hand, expected to resume his official residence and at least to try to go on governing the province as before.

The immediate difficulty was practical: the city was too small to handle two first-class receptions—two parades, along two routes of march, both thronged with cheering citizens—at one time. Broadway, from Fort George on the south to the Commons on the north, was the only street suitable for a proper parade, and Colonel John Lasher's Independent Battalion was the city's only militia unit adequate to, and properly uniformed for, ceremonial duty. A considerable number of New Yorkers wished to attend both receptions. Washington had become America's most talked-about celebrity but hardly anyone in New York knew him; whatever their enthusiasm for his cause, many men wanted to see what he was like and to wish him well, and some imagined that an acquaintance with the general might in the future prove to be advantageous. As for Tryon, his personal popularity was as high as it had been before his trip, and the hundreds of New Yorkers who worked or had worked for the British felt obliged to be on hand to welcome him back.

New York wished to impress Washington without offending the governor, so the Provincial Congress had worked out a desperate plan to keep Washington's welcome uptown and Tryon's downtown, hoping to keep the two from clashing in midtown. Most of Lasher's battalion was held near the Commons, about halfway between the Hoboken Ferry landing near the west end of present-day Canal Street, where Washington was expected, and Coenties Slip near the southern tip of the island, where Tryon was to disembark. Lasher's orders were to keep alert and to proceed, on the double, to greet whichever dignitary arrived first—in the hope that they would not arrive simultaneously.

Tryon's tact enabled this unlikely arrangement to succeed to a certain extent. While the governor waited on board his ship, the *Juliana,* for New York to get ready to receive him, several of his friends, including Edmund Fanning, sailed out to visit him. They told Tryon the whole story of New York's embarrassing predicament, and the governor, with great consideration, postponed his landing time by four hours until 8 P.M. That took the worst of the pressure off New York. Washington arrived about 4 but stopped for an hour at Leonard Lispenard's mansion near the ferry landing; by the time the general was ready to proceed south to Hull's Tavern near Trinity Church, where he was staying, Lasher's men were there, ready to march at the head of the parade. Although the party for the general was not quite over by eight o'clock, those New Yorkers who had attended but wanted to greet the governor too were able to leave Hull's Tavern without seeming to hurry and walk the few blocks to the foot of Broad Street to join the good-sized gathering at Coenties Slip.

In its relief that the day had been no worse, New York did not understand how poor an impression it had made upon Washington. He had arrived full of suspicions about New York's devotion to the war effort, as it had become. At Lispenard's, Washington had received his first full account of the fighting that had taken place on Charleston Neck a week earlier in a letter from the Massachusetts Provincial Congress. It was disheartening. Breed's Hill, Bunker's Hill, and all the rest of the Neck were lost to the British; and the one consolation was that the Americans had forced the British to pay a high price in soldiers' lives. It was almost unbelievable, Washington thought, that under these circumstances any New Yorker would want to welcome Tryon back.

Quite a few men, including most of the members of the Governor's Council who had not already sailed from New York, did call on Tryon to pay their respects. They all hoped that Tryon could do something helpful before the conflict got worse, but Tryon's own discouragement was almost total. His gout was no better. He had no troops at his command because they had all been shifted to Boston. He had no new instructions from London that made sense, no ideas about anything he could do, and, apart from soldierly habit, no ambition to succeed in his mission.

The next day, Monday, June 26, the New Yorkers made matters worse. The Provincial Congress was eager to present testimonial addresses to Washington and the two generals with him, Charles Lee and Philip Schuyler, the latter having just been made commander of the Continental army's New York Department. Even though Washington and Lee were anxious to get to Cambridge as quickly as they could and Schuyler was anxious to get to his headquarters in Albany, the commander in chief agreed to delay their departures until the afternoon, mostly in order to avoid hurting New York's feelings.

New York's address to General Washington was absurd. It was honest, but its authors had tried to include something to please each of the many shades of opinion represented in the Provincial Congress. Almost every affirmation was balanced by a negation, starting with the tortured introduction:

> At a time when the most loyal of His Majesty's subjects, from a regard to the laws and constitution by which he sits on the throne, feel themselves reduced to the unhappy necessity of taking up arms to defend their dearest rights and privileges; while we deplore the calamity of this divided Empire, we rejoice in the appointment of a gentleman from whose abilities we are taught to expect both security and peace. . . .[2]

Thus the address wound along, heading first this way and then that, until it made an insulting request: could Washington promise that when the fighting was over he would resign "cheerfully" as commander in chief and "reassume the character of our worthiest citizen"?

If Washington *had* had secret ambitions to become a postwar military dictator, he would not have confessed everything in response to New York's naïve question. Instead of taking offense, Washington thanked New York for the welcome it had given him, and provided the Provincial Congress exactly the sentence it wanted to hear:

> When we assumed the soldier, we did not lay aside the citizen; and we shall most sincerely rejoice with you in that happy hour when the establishment of American liberty, upon the most firm and solid foundations, shall enable us to return to our private stations in the bosom of a free, peaceful, and happy country.[3]

2. Entry for June 26, 1775, *Journals of the Provincial Congress, Province Convention, Committee of Safety and Council of Safety of the State of New York 1775–1777* (Albany: Thurlow Weed, 1842).

3. *Ibid.*

6

The War Reaches New York

WASHINGTON rode away from New York even more distrustful than he had been on his arrival. Most of a year went by before he understood that New York was at least as dedicated as any other colony to winning the war. The Provincial Congress was late in instructing its delegates in Philadelphia to vote in favor of the Declaration of Independence, a point that has been held against New York to this day. But the delay occurred partly because the Provincial Congress, concerned about knowing exactly how all the counties felt about the question, called two county-by-county elections to test local sentiments.

General Washington had to learn that New York was not Virginia, or Massachusetts, or Connecticut. All of New York's political efforts were marked by legal complexities that could easily be mistaken for bad faith. The merchants and lawyers in the Provincial Congress and representing New York in Philadelphia were anything but simple-minded. They were dealing with complicated issues, and working hard; and they were not inclined toward rhetoric unless it was absolutely necessary. They preferred not to take extreme positions (all of New York's most successful merchants were adroit at hedging the great risks involved in almost every trading venture) and they searched patiently for compromise as a matter of professional habit. On many occasions when the New York Provincial Congress appeared hesitant, it was simply waiting for a subcommittee to find the facts and to determine, if possible, what the future was likely to bring.

From the British point of view New York was the key to the war strategy, the main target of the powerful military effort King George directed against his North American colonies. For a few months at the very beginning, Lord Dartmouth, the Colonial Secretary, hoped to smash the rebellion around Boston before it spread. After that plan failed, the basic British idea was to capture New York City and, using it as a base, to take control of the rivers-and-lakes waterway between the St. Lawrence and the Atlantic. Thus the colonies would be split approximately in two. London assumed that the British navy could prevent the rebels from supporting each other by sea. This divide-and-conquer scheme looked better on the map than on the ground: the Hudson River, Lake George, Lake Champlain, and the Richelieu River formed a neat dotted line, but cutting along it in order to isolate New England proved difficult.

The Americans indulged themselves for a time in a related fantasy: that Canada, with its predominantly French population, might like to become a "fourteenth colony" and join its neighbors in the fight against the British. In that unrealistic hope, Washington's first active military campaign, undertaken in combination with his static effort to keep the British bottled up in Boston, was a Canadian invasion. In May 1775 Ethan Allen and Benedict Arnold had opened the way for Schuyler to march north by capturing the British fort at Ticonderoga, but the Continental Congress opposed a further advance for the time being. It changed its mind at the end of June, while Washington, Lee, and Schuyler were trying to avoid being overwhelmed by the Provincial Congress's hospitality. Hardly any of the necessary preparations had been made, and it was August before the advance began with General Richard Montgomery, Schuyler's second-in-command, leading the way. (Schuyler, by then, was ill and discouraged.) Washington doubled the stakes. Why not capture Quebec as well as Montreal? While Montgomery, who started with about 1,200 men and a makeshift fleet, was struggling to take the strongpoints on the Richelieu, St. Johns, and Chambly, a second column of 1,100 men under Arnold made its way up the Kennebec River and then down the Chaudière, with Quebec as its objective. For lack of communications, the leaders in Cambridge, New York, and Philadelphia were unable to monitor the progress of the two-pronged attack or prepare themselves for the appalling defeat that was in the making.

Montgomery captured Montreal on November 13. That news, delivered by riders to Albany and New York City, seemed encouraging: the entire dotted line was for the moment under American control. If the British wanted to move south along the same route, they would surely find the going difficult. But the American line was thin indeed. New York's recruiting quota for the Continental army that summer had been four regiments, or 3,080 men and officers. The province had raised about half that number, with difficulty, and nearly all of them had gone north to take part at one place or another in Montgomery's advance. When Montgomery moved on from Montreal in order to help Arnold at Quebec, Montgomery had scarcely 400 men present and fit for duty: disease and disaffection had been far more destructive than the Canadian or British opposition. By the time Arnold reached the banks of the St. Lawrence, opposite Quebec, the rigors of his heroic long march had reduced his column to no more than 700 men. Montgomery lost another 100 men on his way from Montreal to Quebec. When the combined American force attacked the fortified city on the last day of 1775, it contained no more than 1,000 soldiers. Instead of outnumbering General Guy Carleton's defending troops by three to one, as the military rule of thumb would have prescribed, the Americans were themselves outnumbered by something like two to one.

The attack failed badly. Not only did Carleton hold Quebec, but he inflicted heavy, demoralizing casualties on the Americans. Montgomery was killed, as were two aides. Arnold was seriously wounded. Months went by before the full extent of the American losses could be pieced together: 60 killed or wounded, and 426 taken prisoner. Foolhardy though the attack may have been, the reports of the defeat shocked New York Province. New York's regiments had all participated in the campaign, and almost all of the men with Montgomery at Quebec had belonged to the First New York Regiment. An agonizing period of waiting to know whether a man was alive or not, or well, or taken prisoner fell upon families throughout the province.

Almost overnight the victories of late 1775 turned sour, and what had seemed like a degree of security on the north disappeared. Did the expedition have any strength left? Could the Americans prevent the British from reversing the direction of the action and attacking New York, New Hampshire, and Massachusetts along the routes Montgomery and Arnold had taken? The answer was no. Ten months later, in October 1776, General Carleton, heavily reinforced, was at St. Johns planning to attack down Lake Champlain and the upper Hudson to Albany.

The New York Provincial Congress was profoundly affected by the Canada fiasco. The terrible seriousness of the war had not been quite so plain except, perhaps, briefly on the night of August 23, 1775. On that occasion the British battleship *Asia,* anchored in the East River off the foot of Wall Street, had fired a thunderous broadside over the city's rooftops toward Fort George to stop a work party of soldiers from stealing the fort's cannon. That had reminded the Provincial Congress and all of New York that British seapower—represented by the *Asia* and a sloop of war, the *Kingfisher,* which had been standing guard over the harbor since July—was capable of wiping out the capital of the province at will. The *Asia* had fired solid shot that had not done much danger; the roofs of Roger Morris's town house and Fraunces's Tavern had been torn open and half a dozen smaller buildings on Whitehall Street had been damaged, and three or four New Yorkers were wounded, but no one was killed. If the *Asia* had wanted to destroy the city, it would have used firebombs. Given New York's highly inflammable construction, a few broadsides could have reduced the place to ashes.

Still, the broadside at three o'clock in the morning, which had been preceded by several warning shots, had started a panic. Many New Yorkers mistook the sound of the alarm drums for a signal that the British were invading Manhattan. Some of them ran into the streets, where they found that nobody knew what was happening. Others made for their cellars.

NEW YORK CITY IN 1776

Adapted from Holland's Plan of the City of New York, 1776

Quarter of a Mile

A. Military Hospital
B. Governor's House
C. Secretary's Office
D. Custom House
E. Fish Market
F. Old Slip Market
G. Meat Market
H. Fly Market
I. Peck's Market
K. Oswego Market
L. Exchange
M. Dutch Free School
N. Engine which supplies
   the city with fresh water
O. St. Paul's
P. Trinity Church
Q. St. George's Chapel
R. Old Dutch Church
S. New Dutch Church
T. Lutheran Church
V. Calvinist Church
W. French Protestant Church
X. Quakers' Meeting
Y. Presbyterian Meeting
Z. Baptist Meeting
a. Moravian Meeting
b. New Lutheran Meeting
c. Jews' Synagogue

EAST RIVER OR THE SOUND

NORTH OR HUDSON RIVER

DELANCEY'S SQUARE

ROAD TO ALBANY & BOSTON

MARSHY GROUND

Fresh Water Pond

Jews' Burying Ground

COMMON

THE FORT

BATTERY

Hundreds tried to flee to New Jersey or Brooklyn on the ferries, which were immediately overwhelmed by the traffic, or north on the island to the countryside. Many tried to take their valuables with them in wagons or carts, creating insoluble jams in the narrow streets. Most of the refugees were unable to get far and realized by daylight that they had no place to hide—at least none that they could afford.

To a remarkable extent, however, New York recovered from the *Asia*'s bombardment. Governor Tryon, who had spent the night visiting friends on Long Island, hurried back to New York and arranged a preposterous conference the following morning—a joint meeting of members of the Governor's Council, the Corporation of the City, members of the New York Provincial Congress, and members of the New York City Committee. (Officially, Tryon was not supposed to admit that these last two bodies existed.) Thanks to Tryon's diplomacy, these mismatched conferees arranged a compromise. Tryon offered to let the stolen guns stay where they were, on the Commons parade ground, provided that they were not moved any farther away from where they belonged. The New Yorkers agreed, on their part, that the royal navy warships, including the *Asia*, could continue to buy fresh provisions in the New York City markets—as much bread, butter, meat, cheese, along with rum, wine, beer, and ale as they could pay for.

After the Canadian news was absorbed, the contradiction of provisioning the British in New York harbor while Montgomery was in the very act of moving north on Lake Champlain on his way to the Richelieu River and Montreal became embarrassing. But the majority of New Yorkers were not yet ready to concede that England's use of military force against her obstreperous American colonies made separation almost inevitable—assuming, that is, that the colonies could win. The prevailing opinion in the Provincial Congress and in the New York delegation to the Continental Congress was that negotiation followed by reconciliation was still possible.

New York's unrealistic view was widely shared. As late as January 15, 1776, Sam Adams of the Massachusetts delegation, who had long thought that the time to part had arrived, maneuvered adroitly to postpone a Continental Congress debate on the desirability of making separation a war aim. If a vote were taken, Adams feared, the proposal would lose. The accuracy of Adams's sense of the meeting was almost immediately borne out when the Continental Congress put a special committee, headed by James Wilson of Pennsylvania, to work writing a declaration of *non*-independence. (By February 14, when the six-thousand-word document was finished, a formal declaration against independence seemed rather pointless. Congress voted to table the Wilson committee document.)

The news from England was reaching New York nearly three months late, and then it took another day or two to get to Philadelphia; no man in either city understood that the king, his ministers, and Parliament had ordered the level of force raised to an awe-inspiring, unprecedented degree, or that the full weight of the massive attack was to fall first on New York. Lord George Germain had established himself as managing director of the war effort. He was withdrawing the British from Boston to Halifax in order to get his regiments ready for the new assault; he had completed successful negotiations with several of the German states to provide mercenaries; and he was prodding Admiral Sir Hugh Palliser to get 52,000 tons of troop transports ready to sail for New York no later than April 7. Germain wanted the new divisions with their naval support and the Halifax forces, rested and refurbished, to meet in the lower harbor off Sandy Hook before the end of June, wind and weather permitting.

Not knowing any of this, New York worked diligently on preparations to defend Manhattan Island and Brooklyn against troop landings and to obstruct the Hudson River. General Washington, who had anticipated the British strategy, sent General Lee, his brilliant, erratic assistant, to speed the preparations along. Lee succeeded to some extent, although he wasted time hunting for Tories in rural Queens without catching a soul who could give aid and comfort to the enemy. There were several hundred British sympathizers hiding out on the south shore of Long Island waiting to join the British when they arrived, but Lee couldn't find them.

Lee refrained from explaining to New York what he fully appreciated: that the only way to keep New York City out of the hands of the British was to burn it to the ground. Britain's overwhelming naval strength—more than one hundred ships compared to the Colonies' eight—enabled the British to move as they pleased against the flanks and rear of any American force that attempted to hold the southern tip of Manhattan. The Americans had a better chance of keeping the British from using the Hudson to sail to Albany, and they were working on several schemes to block the channel by sinking weighted ships and by stringing chains across it. In the Highlands, where the river is narrow from Stony Point almost as far north as Newburgh, the New Yorkers muffed their good chance of controlling the double right-angle turn past West Point by laboring to fortify the low-lying island on the east shore instead of the high ground on the opposite side, where the Military Academy now stands.

On March 17 the British withdrew from Boston. On March 29 the main body of the Continental army, one group of units at a time, began the twelve-day march to New York City. General Washington himself, with Adjutant General Horatio Gates, their aides, and Washington's detachment of guards, arrived at New York City on April 13. Within a few weeks, to his surprise, Washington realized that his poor opinion of New York had been formed too hastily. In their own fashion, New Yorkers were as devoted to the Continental Association's success as the New Englanders or the Virginians. The New Yorkers' pursuit of success simply followed a different style. Their greatest efforts were directed, locally, to an unobtainable goal: denying the port and the city of New York to the Howe brothers, Admiral Richard and General William.

New York City was militarily indefensible, but the political implications of burning it down without a fight were ominous. If after a whole year the Continental army could do no better than default on the defense of New York City, the cause would surely seem hopeless to many Americans. Yet Lee, the architect of New York's defensive lines and fortifications, assumed that the city was doomed; he was only trying to make Brooklyn and Manhattan into "a disputable field of battle"—meaning that he hoped to make the British pay dearly in casualties.

The British arrived on schedule in late June and early July: the largest expeditionary force Great Britain had ever assembled, including some 32,000 well-trained professional soldiers, completely armed and equipped and supported by ten ships of the line, twenty frigates, and one hundred seventy transports of various sizes. On July 2 and 3, the British occupied Staten Island without meeting any opposition and the New York Provincial Congress moved from City Hall to the courthouse in White Plains, although a week elapsed before a legal quorum—a majority of the counties—was present and ready to vote. New York had stopped in the middle of its clear and present dangers to hold a new set of county-by-county elections for Provincial Congress delegates, hoping to make sure that the legislature accurately represented the voters' sentiments. It was the second such election within a month, and the issues were not so clear as the New Yorkers might have wished.

Nevertheless, when the new Provincial Congress convened at White Plains on July 9, the delegates had no difficulty in voting that New York Province should become an independent state with a government of its own, or in approving the Declaration of Independence that the Continental Congress had passed (New York abstaining) on July 2. The resolution of approval was in the form of a report by a committee that John Jay headed, and it was in Jay's handwriting, with the heading at the top of the page: "In Convention of the Representatives of the State of New York, White Plains, July 9, 1776." The first paragraph, lumping the issues of statehood and independence together in fifty-eight words, was the heart of the matter. It read:

> Resolved, that the reasons assigned by the Continental Congress for declaring the United Colonies free and independent states are cogent and conclusive; and that while we lament the cruel necessity which has rendered the measure unavoidable, we approve the same, and will, at the risk of our lives and fortunes, join with the other Colonies in supporting it.

Jay might have written "the other states" instead of "the other Colonies." No matter. The resolution passed without a dissenting vote. Five hundred copies of the Declaration of Independence were ordered printed in handbill form to be distributed, along with the announcement that New York had become a free and independent state, in every district of all the counties.

At their retreat formations that evening, the troops in the city and in Brooklyn heard the Declaration's sober arguments read aloud—"the grounds and reasons," as General Washington described them, which, he hoped, would "serve as a fresh incentive to every officer and soldier to act with fidelity and courage." With Staten Island in the enemy's hands, and with the Narrows and the lower bay so filled with British ships that to one observer the scene resembled a wood of trimmed pine trees, Washington expected that the British advance toward Manhattan might begin at any hour, whenever Howe chose. That dreary thought gave extraordinary weight to the document's last sentence: "And for the support of this Declaration, with firm reliance on the Protection of Divine Providence, we mutually pledge to each other our Lives, our Fortunes, and our Sacred Honor."

7

A Small Taste of Success

$\mathcal{U}$NHAPPILY for New York, the British continued their conquest of the seaport with great self-confidence and almost uninterrupted success. At the end of August 1776 Howe took the western end of Long Island, starting at Gravesend Bay, where his troops landed in assault barges they had built on Staten Island. More than a thousand Americans were killed, wounded, or taken prisoner. Only the luck of a strong northeasterly wind saved the other ten thousand by keeping the British warships out of the East River, from which they might have prevented the retreat to Manhattan. All of the survivors were ferried across the East River under cover of darkness and fog on the night of August 29.

The fighting stopped for a few hours on September 11. Major General John Sullivan, who had been taken prisoner in Brooklyn, had understood the Howe brothers to say that they were authorized by the king to offer the colonies generous peace terms. The Continental Congress, looking for information, sent Benjamin Franklin, John Adams, and Edward Rutledge to find out exactly what negotiating powers, if any, the Howe brothers had. It was a waste of time. The congressmen conferred with Admiral Howe by himself—General Howe excused himself from attending because of pressing military duties—in Christopher Billop's handsome old (1695) Staten Island mansion, but the conference confirmed what the Americans had thought all along:

the Howe brothers were empowered to grant pardons to rebels who had changed their minds and were ready to reaffirm their allegiance to the king, but that was all. They could not negotiate a treaty, and the Howes could not even discuss independence.

The next day, September 12, Washington began to withdraw from New York City to Harlem Heights. There he planned to mass almost all that remained of the Continental army in the hope that, for all their weakness and shortcomings, his soldiers could defend the high ground against a British attack from the south. In addition to the losses he had suffered on Long Island, Washington's army was melting away through desertions, especially from the ranks of the "Continental militia"—men who had enlisted for only a few months. Whole regiments had gone home, almost as a body. The eight thousand men in the thirteen Connecticut militia regiments, for example, had dwindled to about two thousand in a week's time.

Washington understood that military prudence called for the complete abandonment of Manhattan. The British fleet was capable of taking an assault force up the Hudson to land almost anywhere north of the Americans, and a landing on the Westchester shore of Long Island Sound was equally possible, perhaps even easier. Should Howe make either move (or a combination of both), he could trap the Continental army, cut it off from any possible retreat, and, given his great superiority in strength, defeat it in his own good time. Yet Washington had decided to try to hold the upper end of the island for an appallingly simple reason: he believed that after their Long Island defeat his troops were too demoralized to execute a major retreat.

Howe ignored his opportunity. Washington had moved about two-thirds of his men to Harlem Heights when the British attacked Manhattan, seemingly more interested in securing the city than in winning the war. On the morning of September 15 five British warships bombarded the shore at Kip's Bay, a shallow cove on the East River between the modern Thirty-second and Thirty-eighth streets, while British and German soldiers were ferried across the river in barges. The thin line of mostly untrained American militiamen who were guarding that part of the shoreline broke and ran. Within an hour, the British had established a firm beachhead, including most of present-day Murray Hill. By mid-afternoon, the second wave of British soldiers landed—nine thousand added to the four thousand in the initial assault force—and before dark New York City was back in British hands. The attack had gone exactly according to Howe's written plans—unfortunately, from a British point of view, because Howe had missed another opportunity. If he had ordered his units to move west out of the beachhead, as well as south and north, the British would almost surely have interrupted the last part of the American withdrawal, a column of five or six thousand men marching toward the Harlem Heights positions and keeping as far to the west as possible in order to avoid an impromptu battle.

Nothing had gone Washington's way, apart from the fact that the withdrawal to Harlem Heights had been completed. He suspected that his army's morale was even lower than before because of the Kip's Bay fiasco. Washington wrote a report to John Hancock, president of the Continental Congress, explaining that he hoped he would be able to defend his Harlem Heights position "if the generality of our troops would behave with tolerable bravery." But, Washington added, "experience, to my extreme affliction, has convinced me that this is rather to be wished for than expected."

Despite that pessimistic observation, the day—September 16—was about to bring Washington a limited victory of just the sort he hoped for. At dawn he sent a reconnaissance party down from Harlem Heights to locate the British forward positions and if possible to discover Howe's immediate intentions. The British lines were about two miles to the south, as the Americans promptly discovered. They involved themselves in a skirmish—although their job was to gather information, not to fight—and when they finally retreated, the British pursued as far as Claremont, the rise that is now the site of Grant's Tomb. Washington's scouting party returned safely to Harlem Heights, but a British bugler, standing on Claremont and facing across the valley (or Hollow Way, as it was then called), made the mistake of blowing the fox-hunting call for the end of the chase. That brassy insult may have helped Washington decide to continue and enlarge the engagement. He planned to lure some of the British down from their high ground into the valley, send a flanking party around the British right using a massive outcropping of rocks for concealment, and attack the British rear. It was the elementary infantry maneuver, to be sure, but it called for more discipline and control than anything the Americans had managed in seventeen months of war.

As in all battles, the plan partly misfired. The British were indeed lured down into the valley by a noisy demonstration directly in front of them, but Washington's flanking party accidentally disclosed its position before it had reached the enemy's rear. Within minutes the two officers leading the attempted encirclement—two of Washington's finest commanders—were casualties. Even so, the flanking party gave a good account of itself. The British were forced back uphill along the approximate line of what is now Broadway. Washington, observing from the Heights, committed most of three additional brigades to the action, raising the total number of Americans involved to about two thousand. At the top of the slope, immediately southeast of Claremont, a large open buckwheat field covered the crown of the hill. The field extended from present-day 120th Street to 116th Street and from Riverside Drive to Broadway or a little farther east. (Barnard College, with some of the Columbia University buildings, now occupies a substantial part of the clearing, and my favorite roller-skating street, Claremont Avenue, runs through it from north to south not far from the middle.)

British reinforcements were on the way. They arrived at the field about noon, the leading elements of regiments that contained nearly five thousand men. For most of the next two hours, the two armies, drawn up in formal battle lines, fought to a standstill. Several of Washington's highest-ranking generals, including Nathaniel Greene, George Clinton, and Israel Putnam, rode back and forth behind the formations of musketmen, shouting encouragement and working to maintain discipline. They were elated by the troops' sudden display of courage and aggressiveness—almost unbelievable by the standards of the day before. The British began to give way. One of his aides rode to report this to Washington, who had remained at his observation post on the Heights. The general told his aide to order the commanders to break off the engagement and withdraw. He did not want his brigades to advance beyond the buckwheat field or risk a larger battle. Washington assumed, correctly, that Howe had ordered up additional reinforcements. Before Washington's orders could be delivered, the British were in full retreat. Some of the Americans, exuberant at the unfamiliar sight of the backs of British uniforms, followed for half a mile—almost to the place where, at daybreak, the fighting had begun.

By late afternoon, the Americans were back on Harlem Heights in the comparative security of their prepared lines. Washington estimated his losses for the day at sixty, including the wounded and missing, but they were considerably greater than that. Howe's casualty figures—14 killed and 157 wounded—also understated the facts. For the Americans, the great difference the day had made was the knowledge that some of the best soldiers in the British forces had been challenged in formal battle on an orthodox battlefield and had been driven from it, despite their superior numbers. One of Washington's officers, Colonel Joseph Reed, wrote of the effect of his success in a letter to his wife: "You can hardly conceive the change it has made in our army. The men have recovered their spirits and feel a confidence which before they had quite lost."[1]

One hesitates to think what might have happened without the buckwheat-field victory. For the near future, there was nothing in store for the Continental army but further retreats and defeats: withdrawal to White Plains; the loss of Fort Washington and the 2,800 men who were left behind to defend it; the fall of Fort Lee on the west bank of the Hudson; and retreats across New Jersey to the far side of the Delaware River. Its next small success was the capture of the Hessian garrison at Trenton on December 26, 1776, and by then Washington had no more than 6,000 men listed as "fit for duty." A week later, after the expi-

1. Quoted in Henry P. Johnston, *The Battle of Harlem Heights* (New York: The Macmillan Company for Columbia University Press, 1897), appendix.

ration of most of his soldiers' enlistments on December 31, the Continental army consisted of no more than 2,000, most of them volunteers who had been talked into staying for just a few extra weeks. The war was as good as lost—or so it seemed—for lack of an American army to fight it.

8

Turning Point

*A*S the British settled into their New York City base of operations, beginning a tenancy that would last for seven years, New York's attention returned to the Hudson River–Lake George–Lake Champlain–Richelieu River water route. The Provincial Congress, renamed the Convention of the State of New York, was forced to move north, first to Fishkill at the end of August and then to Kingston, on the west bank of the river more than half the distance to Albany. A depressing winter lay ahead, with almost nothing but bad news and with most of the state's leaders privately worried—in addition to their public concerns—about the physical safety of their families.

In early November 1776 the British occupied Crown Point, just north of Fort Ticonderoga, but the commander, Sir Guy Carleton, decided—correctly, in all probability—that the season was too late for him to continue south. Instead of driving forward to Ticonderoga and beyond, to link up with General Howe's forces somewhere in the upper Hudson valley, Carleton withdrew his army to Canada, expecting to renew the campaign in the summer of 1777.

In spite of all distractions, the Convention's special committee charged with the responsibility of recommending a new form of government for New York managed to write a draft constitution of some distinction and have it ready for submission to the Convention by the middle of March 1777. Abraham Yates, Jr., of Albany was the committee's chairman, and its membership was a marvel of diversity, for it included the whole spectrum of New York opinion. The committee's deliberations were off the record, but it is assumed that John Jay, Robert R. Livingston, and Gouverneur Morris, along with Yates, were the committee's leaders; and there is no doubt that Jay, in addition to contributing greatly to the formulation of the document, copied the committee's final version in his own hand. After five weeks of spirited debate—as if there were all the time in the world—and considerable amending, the Convention approved New York's first state constitution on April 20, 1777.

It was a conservative document, and the new government it established resembled the old government it was replacing to a surprising degree. New York's founding fathers clearly, and with good reason, feared a despotic state governor, and they were also uneasy about the potential arrogance of a popular assembly that might rule unchecked. The legislature was composed of two houses: an Assembly of seventy county representatives, with each county allotted a quota of seats based on its population and with the assemblymen serving terms of only one year; and a Senate representing "four great districts," drawn especially for the purpose, with its twenty-four members serving for four years. In order to vote for an assemblyman, one had to be a tax-paying freeholder with property worth £20 or a renter paying at least 40 shillings in rent a year. In order to vote for a senator (or the governor, who was chosen by Senate electors), one had to meet a property qualification of £100. As this worked out, there were considerably more voters than there had been before, but not more than half of them were qualified to vote for the higher offices. The governor, whose term ran for three years, now had two councils instead of one. The power to veto the legislature's acts rested in a Council of which the governor was a member together with the chancellor and the judges of the Supreme Court. (Council vetoes could be overridden by two-thirds majorities in both houses.) All important non-elective officers were appointed by the second Council, consisting of the governor and one senator from each of the four districts.

Fittingly enough, the first Chief Justice of the New York

Supreme Court was the extraordinary Mr. Jay, then all of thirty-two years old. (In 1789, President Washington would appoint Jay the first Chief Justice of the United States—after Jay had served as president of the Continental Congress, minister to Spain, peace commissioner to England for the negotiations that ended the war, secretary for foreign affairs in the Confederation years, and ad interim secretary of state until he was relieved by Thomas Jefferson.) By some mysterious chemistry, Jay epitomized one aspect of New York style: the splendid self-confidence of the well-to-do patrician whose deepest concerns are personal rectitude and public service. Jay was the grandson of a Huguenot, related to the Van Cortlandts through his mother, and married to a Livingston. He had "inched reluctantly" toward believing in separation, as historian Richard B. Morris has described the process. After he had made up his mind, however—it may have been late in June 1776—Jay had no further doubts, and his passion for winning the war of independence was at least as great as any Liberty Boy's.

On the day of Jay's appointment, May 3, 1777, the Convention made Robert R. Livingston chancellor of the State of New York, and in June the £100-freeholders made Brigadier General George Clinton, who was on active duty as the officer in charge of the defense of the Highlands, New York's first governor. The Livingstons, along with most of the landed gentry, were surprised. Clinton was a lawyer and reasonably well-to-do, but he did not by any means belong to the top stratum of New York society. He was a radical Whig from Ulster County who represented the wilderness yeomanry, city tradesmen, and artisans. Clinton was dignified, plain-spoken, blunt, with a passion for economy and a loathing for finery. Philip Schuyler, who had come in second in the election, commented: "His family connections do not entitle him to so distinguished a predominance, yet he is virtuous and loves his country, has abilities and is brave." Even though Clinton's election was unexpected, he was destined to serve as governor throughout the war and far beyond: an extraordinary string of six consecutive terms from 1777 to 1792 and then a seventh term starting in 1801.

The state was furnished with a constitution, a government,

and a governor, but as the summer of 1777 grew warmer, there seemed to be hardly any reason to imagine that New York—or any of the other former colonies—would be able to maintain its declared independence. Washington's army had survived the winter in camp at Morristown, New Jersey, and new enlistments had brought his strength up to about 8,000. In June, the British engaged the Americans at several places in New Jersey without any important results. Then Howe withdrew all his troops to New York City and Staten Island.

Washington had to assume that Howe was preparing to move somewhere. According to simple logic, Howe should have been taking his huge army up the Hudson, for, as Washington knew, the British were moving south once more from St. Johns on the way to Ticonderoga and Albany, as General Carleton had expected. The commander of the expedition was not Carleton, however, but General John Burgoyne, who had spent a leave in London persuading the king and his cabinet to give him the assignment. Burgoyne's soldiers called him "Gentleman Johnny" because he treated them reasonably well at a time when military discipline was often brutal. He had 9,000 British and German troops, 400 Indians, and 100 American Tories in his command, a fleet of ships, gunboats, and bateaux for carrying men and supplies, and more than 100 cannon. A much smaller British force, commanded by Colonel Barry St. Leger, moved up the St. Lawrence to Lake Ontario. It was to support Burgoyne's attack by moving from Oswego along the Mohawk to the Hudson.

On paper, it looked as if the British objective of splitting the rebellious colonies in two would succeed. Schuyler had 2,500 Continental soldiers and perhaps 900 militiamen at Ticonderoga, a Continental regiment at Fort Stanwix at the head of the Mohawk valley, and militia detachments at Skenesboro, Fort Anne, Fort Edward, and Albany. They did not seem to be nearly enough. On July 5, Burgoyne's field artillery was in position on Mount Defiance, looking down on Ticonderoga. Major General Arthur St. Clair, in command of the garrison, wisely decided to abandon the overrated fortress, and the Americans retreated down the east side of Lake George, chopping down trees as they moved south to block the roads.

Washington wanted to help Schuyler, but until Howe revealed his intentions Washington could not be certain that Philadelphia was safe. With Ticonderoga fallen, it seemed almost incredible to Washington that Howe was not planning to move up the Hudson to link up with Burgoyne. Yet on July 23 Howe's great fleet, carrying close to 17,000 soldiers, sailed from New York and headed out to sea. Was the sailing a ruse? Was Howe simply trying to draw the Americans to the south before he doubled back on his way to Albany? The tormenting puzzle lasted until, on August 25, Howe's army began landing on the north shore of the Chesapeake Bay with Philadelphia as its objective. Washington hurried south, hoping to block the attack on the unofficial capital of the United States while the Continental Congress began planning to move itself to York, Pennsylvania.

On the Albany front, meanwhile, the British were encountering unexpected difficulties. St. Leger's diversionary attack, which had seemed almost irresistible a month earlier when his 1,700-man force had left Oswego on its way to Fort Stanwix (on the site of present-day Rome), had been stopped. St. Leger had started with 350 British and Hessian regulars, close to 1,000 Indians led by Iroquois chief Captain Joseph Brant, some Canadian militia, and two Tory units, Sir John Johnson's Royal Greens and Colonel John Butler's Tory Rangers. The Fort Stanwix garrison, commanded by twenty-eight-year-old Colonel Peter Gansevoort, consisted of only 550 men of the 3rd New York Continentals.

When St. Leger reached Fort Stanwix on August 2, he half expected that the mere sight of his well-equipped columns would persuade Colonel Gansevoort to surrender. St. Leger was wrong. A fifty-year-old local landowner, Nicholas Herkimer, a brigadier general in the militia whose family had emigrated to the Mohawk valley from the Rhenish Palatinate and who had served as chairman of the Tryon County Committee of Safety, was marching toward Fort Stanwix with 800 volunteers, hoping to assist Gansevoort. Six miles from the fort, at a village called Oriskany, Herkimer's mile-long column marched into an Indian ambush that St. Leger had arranged. The savage six-hour hand-to-hand fight that followed may have been the bloodiest encounter in proportion to the numbers engaged of the entire war. Herkimer was fatally wounded, and none of the reinforcements got through to Fort Stanwix. Herkimer's efforts helped Gansevoort in another way: during the Oriskany battle, when the British camp was nearly empty, Gansevoort's able second-in-command, Lieutenant Colonel Marinus Willet, had led a highly successful raid upon it and had made off with twenty-one wagonloads of muskets, ammunition, and assorted supplies.

News of Oriskany reached General Schuyler at Stillwater, just north of Albany. Although Burgoyne's army had reached Fort Edward on the Hudson—only twenty-four miles away—on July 29, Schuyler was determined to help Gansevoort. Most of Schuyler's officers disagreed; they felt that the army in front of Albany already had as much as it could do without reinforcing Fort Stanwix, 110 miles to the west, and the New Englanders in Schuyler's command all but accused him of wanting to neglect their region in order to protect his own. Schuyler was also in trouble with the Continental Congress for having lost Ticonderoga. He was outraged by these criticisms and insinuations, and he announced that he would personally accept responsibility for sending relief to Fort Stanwix. Schuyler called for a brigadier general to command the relief expedition. Benedict Arnold, a major general and Schuyler's second in command, volunteered. Arnold set off at once with 950 men and, by spreading the word ahead, convinced several hundred of St. Leger's Indians that a huge army was marching to Gansevoort's rescue. Some of the Indians mutinied. The chiefs of the Indians who stayed insisted that St. Leger order a retreat—and, since the Indians were at least half of St. Leger's total strength, he had no choice. By the evening of August 23, when Arnold reach Fort Stanwix, the British were gone.

Meanwhile, Schuyler was replaced on August 19 by Horatio Gates, who had been Schuyler's subordinate in the Northern Department. General Gates, a former English officer who had lived in Virginia before the war and had won Washington's approval and friendship, was ambitious and able; but army administration, rather than field command, was his forte. General

Schuyler was primarily the victim of New England factionalism, but his shortcomings as a field commander could not be denied.

Nevertheless, before Gates relieved Schuyler the latter's successes, combined with Burgoyne's errors, had really ruined Burgoyne's chances of success. St. Clair's decision to abandon Ticonderoga had been correct. The British had exhausted themselves in their struggle south from Skenesboro to Fort Edward because Schuyler had made the obstacles ten times worse than Nature. St. Leger's diversion had been obliterated. Burgoyne's 185-mile supply line between Montreal and Fort Edward was quite unmanageable, as his ill-fated raid on Bennington, Vermont, in search of provisions made evident. The American militiamen were rising to arms at a rapid rate, and some first-class Continental units—Daniel Morgan's "Corps of Rangers, newly formed," for example, which General Washington had sent north just before the Philadelphia campaign—were arriving on the scene. Had Burgoyne been a more experienced general, he might have retreated from Fort Edward as Carleton had withdrawn in 1776, in order to save his army and fight again. But Burgoyne's orders called for him to take Albany, and he still entertained a faint hope that Howe would provide support from the south.

Since Albany was on the west bank of the Hudson and a crossing would be more difficult the farther he moved south, Burgoyne elected to cross the river, using "a bridge of boats," at Saratoga. He started across on the 13th of September. The day before, the Americans had picked Bemis Heights, overlooking the river road on the west side of the Hudson, as the place to dig in and resist Burgoyne's attack. Bemis Heights was about ten miles south of Saratoga (now Schuylerville), and as a strongpoint it had a serious fault: there was still higher ground immediately to its west. If Burgoyne could take the higher ground, his gunners would be able to shoot down from above into the American trenches. (As the Americans had shown at Fort Constitution, Fort Ticonderoga, and elsewhere, they were having difficulty with the concept of seizing the high ground before the enemy did.)

The first battle of Saratoga took place on September 19. The British, divided into three sections, marched south toward Gates's camp on Bemis Heights, where the Americans were reasonably well entrenched. For once the Americans outnumbered the British, by about 7,000 to 4,500. For nearly three hours, while Burgoyne worked to coordinate his three-pronged attack, Gates did nothing. Arnold, who had returned from Fort Stanwix in time to fight at Saratoga, begged Gates to seize the initiative by attacking; and finally Gates did order Morgan's riflemen and Henry Dearborn's light infantry to move forward. If they ran into trouble, Arnold's division would give them support. All afternoon a furious fight raged around the twenty cleared acres in the woods. At the end of the day, after they had returned to their prepared lines, the Americans considered that they had won a victory: their casualties had been only half as many as Burgoyne's. On the other hand, the British had won the battlefield, and there they camped.

More than two weeks passed before Burgoyne renewed the attack. On September 21 Burgoyne got a letter from Lieutenant General Sir Henry Clinton, whom Howe, on his way to Philadelphia, had left behind to guard New York City, in which Clinton offered to help Burgoyne by making a diversionary attack against the Highlands. Burgoyne replied that "an attack or even the menace of an attack upon Fort Montgomery must be of great use, as it will draw away part of their force. . . . Do it, my dear friend, directly."[1] Burgoyne then waited until October 7 before he renewed the Saratoga offensive, not knowing that between October 3 and October 7 Clinton was successfully attacking and capturing not only Fort Montgomery but Fort Clinton and Fort Constitution as well. Clinton's diversionary attack worried Gates a good deal, but in practical terms it had almost no effect on the situation at the Saratoga battlefield. In the meantime, on September 26, General Howe had captured Philadelphia; then, on October 4, Washington had attempted to redeem himself by attacking Germantown, only to be repulsed.

---

1. Quoted in Gerald Howson, *Burgoyne at Saratoga* (New York: Times Books, 1979), p. 214.

The commander in chief had lost the largest city in the United States, and the British had outmaneuvered the Americans with consummate ease. Yet, in a backhanded way, there were compensations. Symbolically, the loss of Philadelphia had seemed unthinkable—in a class with the idea of the loss of Ticonderoga—and yet, as the days went by, the defeat seemed much less devastating than the Americans had expected. Instead of being crushed, the morale of Washington's troops improved. The soldiers felt that they had *almost* won a victory at Germantown, an interpretation that the facts hardly confirmed. They felt better about themselves. World opinion tended to agree with Washington's army. The fact that the Americans had been able to recover quickly from a series of painful defeats, and to summon up the will to make the Germantown counterattack, was impressive. General Howe, who was among those impressed, pulled back from Germantown to Philadelphia and began barricading the city against the possibility of another American attack.

Burgoyne, like Carleton before him, feared that bad weather was about to keep him from capturing Albany. He sent a strong reconnaissance party of 1,500 British soldiers to see whether the American left was approachable; if so, Burgoyne intended to attack in full force the following day. The Americans had improved their position: the high ground on their left, which had been Burgoyne's objective on September 19, had been fortified and strongly occupied. And Gates had learned something: this time, as soon as the British movement was detected, Gates quickly ordered Morgan's riflemen and Enoch Poor's brigade "to begin the game." Both ends of the British line were beaten back, and Burgoyne sent his aide, Sir Francis Clarke, to order a general retirement. Clarke was shot down and captured before he had delivered the command.

Gates and Arnold had been quarreling since the first battle, a complicated clash that had started when Gates, writing his formal report to the Continental Congress, had failed to mention Arnold's name. Gates had relieved Arnold of his command, but Arnold had stayed in the camp, entirely without military status, brooding over his idleness and his disgrace. Now, as the British moved back toward the shelter of their own lines, Arnold could not stand his inactivity any longer. He dashed into the fight, riding his great brown horse. Gates, fearing that Arnold ''might do some rash thing,'' sent an aide to order him back to camp, but the sight of the aide only made Arnold ride faster. The first soldiers Arnold met—part of Poor's brigade—were militia from Norwich, Connecticut, Arnold's home town. They gave their old general a rousing cheer, and Arnold raced on. He overtook the leading regiments of General Ebenezer Learned's brigade, called on them to follow him, and led a charge against the Hessians in the middle of the British line. The assault failed, but the Americans returned and forced the Hessians to retreat. The British attempted to form a second line, but their commander, General Simon Fraser, as inspiring a field officer as Arnold, was picked off by one of Morgan's riflemen. At Fraser's fall, British resistance ended, and the whole line retreated behind their camp's breastworks. Some fifty minutes had elapsed since the first shot was fired.

That seemed to be the end of the battle, but Arnold was not done. He wanted a smashing victory, and he seized the opportunity to attack the British entrenchments. With parts of two of the American brigades, he smashed through the abatis at one point, but the British defense held. Then he rode straight across the line of heavy fire toward the British right, exposing himself to what seemed certain death. He organized another attack on a redoubt occupied by 200 German soldiers under Lieutenant Colonel Heinrich von Breymann. Arnold rode around to the back of the redoubt and entered the sally port. His horse was shot and Arnold was hit in the leg with a bullet that broke his thigh bone. Breymann had been mortally wounded in the attack, and his small force gave up the redoubt. Arnold was carried off the field on a litter—victorious, but lamed for life.

The loss of Breymann's redoubt opened the British camp to attacks on the flank and in the rear. The fighting was over for the day, and during the night Burgoyne, realizing that his position was untenable, withdrew his army. The American losses were about 150. Burgoyne had lost four times that many and all ten of the cannon he had moved forward on the morning of the battle. A week later, on October 13, with the unanimous agreement of his officers, Burgoyne decided he should treat for surrender on honorable terms.

The Saratoga victory is invariably described as "the turning point" of the war of the Revolution, and it was. That does not mean that the Continental army changed from losing to winning—although there were a considerable number of American victories between Saratoga and Yorktown. It does mean that the French, on learning of Burgoyne's and St. Leger's defeats and the positive side of Washington's defeat at Germantown, were persuaded that the United States were capable of sustaining their effort. That made an open alliance between France and the United States practical. (Secret aid from France had been reaching the United States since the summer of 1776.) Without the French money, soldiers, sailors, guns, and ships that sustained the American war effort during the four years from 1777 to 1781, independence could hardly have been achieved.

9

New York Recovers

*T*HE war ended with the Treaty of Paris in September 1783, but the last British units did not leave their New York City base until November 25—Evacuation Day, New Yorkers called it, and a joyous holiday for many years thereafter. It is a fair guess that New York suffered more in the war for independence than did any of the other states. Nearly one-third of all the fighting took place on New York soil. After Burgoyne's failure, the British continued their attacks on New York's frontier settlements year after year, with the usual result that another town—German Flats (now Herkimer), Unadilla, Cherry Valley, Harpersfield, Johnstown, Canajoharie, to name just a few—was burned to the ground. For the most part the British used Indians and American Tories for these guerrilla raids, and many of them were exceedingly wise in the ways of the frontier wilderness: they struck quickly and hard before the settlers could organize a defense.

The British raids were savage, and when the Americans retaliated they were at least equally savage. In 1779, Washington sent Major General John Sullivan on an expedition through the Six Nations' well-developed country from south of Elmira through the Finger Lakes region to the Genesee valley. Washington wrote Sullivan that he wanted the district not "merely overrun but destroyed," and Washington got his wish. When Sullivan was done he reported that he had destroyed forty Indian towns along his line of march as well as 160,000 bushels of

80

corn and a "vast quantity" of vegetables of every kind, but that he had not taken any prisoners (partly from lack of opportunity).

New York City and the surrounding countryside for thirty miles in every direction were completely upset by the insatiable demands of the British garrison and fleet, which transformed the area into a no-man's-land where nobody and nothing was safe. Perhaps one-third of the city burned in numerous small and two great fires (September 21, 1776, and August 3, 1778). The first of these, which started near the fort and swept up the West Side almost to St. Paul's Chapel, destroyed Trinity Church and nearly five hundred other buildings, a major part of the most fashionable part of town; and it seems probable that it was set by patriots bent on executing the scorched-earth policy that the Continental Congress and General Washington had hated to consider.

About one-fourth of the city's population—5,000 of 20,000—tried to stay where they were after General Howe's arrival. Some of them were British sympathizers. A great many more were the poor and the fairly poor, who could not afford to move. As soon as the British had taken firm control—almost immediately—the city became the refuge for Tories from the surrounding countryside and from many of the other states. At its height, the wartime population approached 35,000—10,000 more than ever before. Civilians were reduced to living in shacks and tents; price-gouging was unconscionable. Although the John Street Theatre, which the Provincial Congress had closed, was reopened by the British officers as "The Garrison Dramatic Club," featuring plays written and acted by General Sir Henry Clinton's talented aide, Captain (later Major) John André, almost every other aspect of living was spoiled or degraded.

A particular horror, kept mostly out of sight, was the suffering of the American prisoners of war and crews of captured American vessels who were confined under appalling conditions in the jails on the Commons and in the City Hall, in the King's College buildings, in the Van Cortlandt, Rhinelander, and Liberty Street sugar houses, in the Brick, Middle Dutch, North Dutch, and French churches, and—the worst, by far—in the British prison ships *Jersey, Hunter, Stromboli,* and *Scorpion.*

According to one estimate, the number of prisoners who died on the prison ships during the course of the war was between 7,000 and 11,000—more, in any case, than the total number of Americans who died on the battlefield.

During the long interval between the end of the fighting and formal peace, thousands of American Tories, fearful of what would happen when the protection of the British army was withdrawn, followed those who had left the country earlier. They went to the British Isles, Nova Scotia, Halifax, Montreal and Quebec, Bermuda, the Bahamas, and the West Indies, among other places. In April 1783, a single convoy took 7,000 refugees to Nova Scotia. By Evacuation Day, the city's population was not much more than 10,000 or 12,000. One might think that the patriot New Yorkers who had been leaving the city throughout 1775–1776, as one alarm after another had frightened the residents, might have returned at the earliest opportunity, but only a few did. Seven years was long enough for this other kind of refugee to have put down roots elsewhere, especially in the Hudson River valley, upstate New York, New Jersey, and western Connecticut.

As the last of the British embarked, some 800 American soldiers—all that remained of the Continental army—marched down to the Battery and raised the Stars and Stripes. General Washington, Governor Clinton, General Henry Knox (Washington's remarkable self-taught artillery chief), a number of other officers, and members of the State Convention took possession of the city with a formal procession. Before Washington left for Philadelphia to resign his commission as promised, he gave a party for his officers in the long room of Sam Fraunces's Tavern at Broad and Pearl streets, where a reconstruction of the building stands today. The general, almost overcome with emotion, offered a farewell toast to his comrades: "With a heart full of love and gratitude, I now take leave of you. I most devoutly wish that your latter days may be as prosperous and happy as your former ones have been glorious and honorable."[1]

1. Quoted in Douglas Southall Freeman, *George Washington*, 7 vols. (New York: Charles Scribner's Sons, 1949–1957), 5:467.

Both the city and the state of New York recovered from the
war rather quickly, given the infinite variety of dislocations the
conflict had caused. Immigrants arrived in increasing numbers
especially from New England and from abroad, Ireland in particular and quite a few from France and Germany. Vast tracts of
land in western and northern New York were opened up and
began to be settled by freeholding farmers. Wealthy speculators
in all the cities along the Atlantic coast and in London, Paris,
and The Hague were dealing in New York real estate.

According to an agreement made in 1768, the Iroquois still
held title to a vast stretch of land west of an imaginary line
drawn north and south between Fort Stanwix and the head of the
Unadilla River; but a few thousand Indians, weakened by their
wartime service with the British, were no match for the super-
charged pressures on their property. By 1784, the Iroquois had
surrendered their claims to lands east of Buffalo Creek, and the
Senecas, Cayugas, and Onondagas had also made vast conces-
sions. By 1790, the Indians had given up almost everything east
of the Genesee River; by 1800, there was hardly any Indian land
left in the entire state.

At the same time, New York was disposing of public lands at
bargain prices, including many of the vast tracts that had formerly belong to the political friends of royal governors During
the late 1780s the land commissioners sold more than 5,500,000
acres in northern and central New York. Many of the soldiers
who had fought for independence had been promised 600-acre
bounties as a reward. The legislature set aside more than
1,500,000 acres in the Finger Lakes district for these veterans, a
"Military Tract" that included what are now Onondaga,
Cayuga, and Cortland and parts of Oswego, Wayne, Schuyler,
and Tompkins counties. (The soldiers were not required to settle
on their land; they could sell their warrants to speculators, and
most of them did so.)

The big investors for the most part wanted to take their profits
as quickly as they could. Great tracts were broken into farm-
sized properties, and tens of thousands of them were sold to ac-
tual settlers. The number of self-employed, independent New
Yorkers who could meet the property qualifications for voting

grew tremendously. The same circumstances obtained in "old" counties like Dutchess and Westchester, where manorial owners had been so powerful: the number of tenants dwindled, the number of farmers who owned their own land escalated. The legislature forbade entail and primogeniture, thus assuring that in time the great manors would be partitioned. Fortunes were lost as well as made in New York land speculation. Robert Morris, "the financier of the Revolution," saw his financial empire collapse in the late 1790s because he was overextended in land investments, though not all of it was New York land. He spent three and a half years in a debtors' prison and never recovered his fortune.

The greatest effect of the new nation's first major land rush was a surprise. Its purpose was money-making, but it served to push New York, in the course of twenty or thirty years, far along the way to a democratic society of free men whose economic fates were in their own hands.

The Confederation—"The United States in Congress Assembled" was the official name—held together, almost miraculously, and its loose association of sovereign states had functioned well enough to win the war. But the 1777 Articles of Confederation had not established a national government. The Congress, with its countless committees and departments, was the only branch. There was no executive, except when Congress was not in session. (Then, instead of a single leader, the executive was a committee of thirteen, one from each state.) There were no national courts to protect citizens' rights or resolve disputes among states. The congressional delegates were elected by their state legislatures and paid by their state treasuries, if they were paid at all. In all important decisions, the states were equal. Each had one vote, so that Rhode Island's view was a match for Massachusetts', and a nay from Delaware canceled a yea from New York. While the defense of the United States was the Confederation's responsibility, it could not draft a soldier or a sailor; it could only request the states to provide their shares of manpower according to rule-of-thumb apportionment. It had no control over banking or currency and had to beg the states for

NEW YORK

A photographer's essay by David Plowden

Photographs in sequence

every penny that went into the common treasury. The United States could make treaties with foreign countries affecting commerce, but it could not regulate trade among the states or between them and other countries, and it had no power to compel a recalcitrant state to do what the central government wanted. In short, the thirteen states were much too sovereign for their common good, and the wonder was that, on the whole, the country was recovering from the war.

In January 1785, after it had met in Princeton, Annapolis, and Trenton, Congress moved to New York City. Serious financial, economic, and diplomatic problems—some caused by the war, some by the war's having ended—suggested that a real national government ought to be established. John Jay wrote to George Washington about his apprehensions, and Washington replied:

> We have errors to correct. We have probably had too good an opinion of human nature in forming our confederation. Experience has taught us that men will not adopt and carry into execution measures best calculated for their own good, without the intervention of a coercive power. I do not conceive that we can exist long as a nation without having lodged somewhere a power which will pervade the whole Union in as energetic a manner as the authority of the state governments extends over the several states.[2]

The power to tax was an immediate necessity. The war debt, foreign and domestic, came to $43,000,000, but the Confederation was far from able to pay the interest charges, let alone the principal. When Congress had suggested that the Articles be amended to allow the Confederation to impose a small duty on certain imports from abroad, the states had not agreed. The government was rushing toward bankruptcy, and most of the state legislatures showed no sign of concern.

Young Alexander Hamilton—twenty-eight, Washington's former aide-de-camp, who had married Philip Schuyler's "most unmercifully handsome" daughter Betsey and had started to practice law in New York City—had been arguing for a strong

2. George Washington, *Writings,* ed. John C. Fitzpatrick, 39 vols. (Washington, D.C.: Government Printing Office, 1931–1944), 28:502.

federal union for some years. He thought that a constitutional convention should be called and an improved charter written. James Madison and George Washington of Virginia were the men who actually set such a movement in motion. Virginia, on their urging, invited all of the states to a meeting at Annapolis, Maryland, in September 1786. Hamilton was there, representing New York, but to Virginia's disappointment only four other states attended. Hamilton proposed another convention for the following spring—the first Monday in May 1787—at Philadelphia. Its sole purpose was to be "the revising" of the Articles of Confederation. Congress, still sitting in New York City, endorsed the meeting, and this time all the states except Rhode Island chose delegates.

The Constitutional Convention, as it was later called, brought together a dazzling collection of the country's most distinguished men. Of the sixty-two, eight had been signers of the Declaration of Independence. Seven had been governors of their states. At least twenty-eight had been in Congress. They were skilled in war, diplomacy, legislation, finance, administration, and commerce: the two Morrises, the two Pinckneys, Franklin, Rutledge, Gerry, Ellsworth, Wilson, Randolph, Wythe, Dickinson, Sherman, along with Madison and Hamilton. Washington was their unanimous choice for president of the meeting. They were practical realists, not the radicals of the early days of the Association. Patrick Henry had been chosen to attend but refused to go because, he said, he "smelled a rat." Sam Adams had not been chosen. Most of the delegates who attended were investors in the public securities that the Confederation had been neglecting.

Instead of revising the old Articles, the Convention produced a new document defining a different governmental arrangement altogether. By the end of the long, hot summer, it had written the present Constitution of the United States—minus the amendments, of course—ready for forwarding to the Congress, which was to submit it to the states for ratification.

Two centuries later, the Constitution looks better to the average American than it did in the fall of 1787. Had it been submitted to a general popular vote it probably would not have been ratified. Opposition to it was prompt and impassioned. New York City newspapers were filled with denunciations of the plan. There were five papers—a daily, a semi-weekly, and three weeklies—and Hamilton, distressed because his fellow New Yorkers were reading primarily the negative side of the argument, persuaded Madison and Jay to help him prepare a series of newspaper pieces that would defend the Constitution and argue that a strong central government was necessary. ("A nation without a national government," Hamilton wrote, "is in my view an awful spectacle."[3])

There were eighty-five articles in the series. Jay wrote five, explaining the proposed Constitution's advantages in the field of foreign relations. Madison's twenty-nine pieces dealt with relationships between the state and the federal government and among the executive, legislative, and judicial branches. Hamilton wrote the rest, a total of fifty-one papers. He composed the first of the sheaf in the cabin of his sloop while sailing down the Hudson from Albany to New York City. Hamilton wrote about the necessity of having a respected, effective, central authority; about the security that could come from a national system of just laws impartially enforced; about the likelihood that trade would improve, and the benefits which could be expected from that. Four of the New York newspapers *The Journal, The Independent Journal,* the *Packet,* and the *Daily Advertiser*—took turns printing the essays, and then they were reprinted in many other papers throughout the States. They were all signed "Publius," to conceal the authors' identities. Collected and published as a book, the articles were entitled *The Federalist,* universally regarded as one of this country's great contributions to political thought; and our Supreme Court has been using it ever since to figure out how our government is supposed to function.

In spite of *The Federalist,* the struggle over ratification was bitter, and nowhere more than in New York. Two clear-cut political factions emerged: the Federalists, with Hamilton as their champion, versus the Anti-Federalists, led by Governor Clinton.

3. Quoted in John C. Miller, *Alexander Hamilton: Portrait in Paradox* (New York: Harper & Brothers, 1959), p. 114.

Both parties were in favor of property rights, law and order, and a national government stronger than the Confederation. The issue that separated the two groups of voters was the Constitution's lack of a specific bill of rights, for the Anti-Federalists feared that otherwise a strong national government might destroy local and individual rights.

New York's ratification convention met at Poughkeepsie on June 17, 1788, divided in the Anti-Federalists' favor, forty-six delegates to nineteen—further testimony to Governor Clinton's political persuasiveness. Still, the Federalists' percentage of the popular vote had been considerably better than that, and the New York press was strongly in favor of Hamilton's point of view. The Federalist minority included some great New York names, including Hamilton, Jay, Robert R. Livingston, and James Duane. On June 21, New Hampshire became the ninth state to ratify, assuring ratification. On July 1, Virginia became the tenth. Finally, on July 26, New York voted thirty to twenty-seven in favor of ratification "in full confidence" that at a later date the other states would endorse the rights amendments New York intended to submit. (That left only North Carolina and Rhode Island, where the voters had similar apprehensions about rights, outside the fold.) A year later, when the first Congress met in New York City, Madison arose in the House of Representatives and proposed twelve amendments of just the sort New York, North Carolina, and Rhode Island wanted. Ten of the twelve were ratified by the states by mid-December 1791, and before then North Carolina (1789) and Rhode Island (1790), feeling relieved that the Constitution was acquiring an explicit Bill of Rights, had accepted it.

In its brief glory as the first capital of the United States under the new Constitution, New York was considerably spruced up, especially Federal Hall at Broad and Wall streets. Washington was inaugurated there on April 30, 1789, on the balcony of the second floor. All the windows and rooftops of all the buildings within viewing range were filled with excited spectators, and the streets were jammed. Washington and Chancellor Livingston, who was to administer the oath, stood close to the balcony's delicately wrought iron railing so that a maximum number of citizens could see the ceremony. Samuel Otis, secretary of the Senate, held a leather-bound Bible on a crimson velvet cushion, and behind Otis, as a kind of backdrop, there was a collection of dignitaries, including Vice President John Adams, Governor Clinton, and Henry Knox, the secretary of war. Washington wore a suit of brown cloth with silver buttons decorated with spread-eagles. He had bought the cloth in Connecticut as part of his campaign to encourage American manufactures. He placed his right hand on the Bible. "Do you solemnly swear," Livingston asked, "that you will faithfully execute the office of President of the United States, and will, to the best of your ability, preserve, protect, and defend the Constitution of the United States?" Considering Washington's record during the past fifteen years, the formality was slightly impertinent, but Washington swore with perfect seriousness that he would do so. "It is done," Livingston said. He turned to the crowd and shouted, "Long live George Washington, President of the United States!" The vast gathering roared its approval.

New Yorkers—especially New York newspaper editors and writers of letters to the editor—had a hand in making some of Washington's first decisions. He had to set a style for the presidency, and he did not know how a president ought to behave. His most trusted colleagues were in considerable disagreement on the question. Since he was the first president in the history of the world, Washington was well aware, his every act set a precedent. Too much pomp and circumstance, reminiscent of the European monarchies, would not do; and neither would false plainness, which might imply that the presidency was just like any other job. How much should a president entertain? Before Martha Washington joined him, Washington kept entertainment to a minimum, just two dull afternoon receptions a week. Yet he felt that he ought to make the presidency "respectable," as he put it; he wanted the country, and the nations of the world, to see that a president amounted to something. After his wife arrived, he began to give elaborate and fairly frequent dinners, with lackeys in attendance and free-flowing claret and champagne. He rode in a handsome carriage drawn by six cream-colored horses, with four servants and two gentleman outriders.

Washington could not possibly win a complete victory. No matter what he did, someone complained. One of the most heated debates concerned his title. A committee of the House of Representatives favored "The President of the United States," as in the Constitution. The Senate did not agree. It recommended "His Highness the President of the United States of America and Protector of the Rights of the Same." John Adams thought that "His Most Benign Highness" sounded about right. In the end, Washington's friend Madison, doubtless at the president's request, forced the Senate and the vice president to drop their extravagant suggestions. On formal occasions, the proper introduction would be: "The President of the United States." Informally, all Washington's old friends would continue to address him, as they had for years, as "General."

In 1790, when the 2nd Congress had adjourned, the federal government moved out of New York City. After protracted debate between those who thought the nation's capital should be in the north and those who favored the south, Hamilton and Jefferson had worked out an ingenious trade-off: the south would get the capital, a new federal town on the Potomac River on 100 square miles of land carved out of Maryland and Virginia, while the north would get Virginia's support for a bill providing that the nation would assume the war debts of the thirteen original states. In October the president selected the site, persuaded the landowners to sell for about $66 an acre, and hired Pierre Charles L'Enfant, a French engineer who had come to America with Lafayette, to plan a proper city. As a consolation prize, Philadelphia was to serve as the interim capital while Washington, D.C., was being built—a period, as it turned out, of ten years.

New York regretted the removal. The city fathers had spent a fortune trying to pull their battered town up to federal standards—the expense of remodeling the old City Hall into Federal Hall had come to nearly $100,000, two-thirds of it in charges beyond the original estimates, which was paid by running a lottery—without conspicuous success. The streets were poorly paved if they were paved at all. The water supply was inadequate, and there was no sewer system: Slaves and servants still disposed of sewage at night by carrying it in tubs and buckets and dumping it into the rivers, and a large part of the garbage was eaten by pigs, who continued to wander around town as they had since Dutch days. Not surprisingly, the first of a series of yellow fever epidemics that was to last for thirty years occurred in 1791.

But those pessimists (of whom there were more than a few) who predicted that New York could not stand its political demotion were undervaluing a number of basics, especially the natural superiority of New York's harbor and the increasing importance of the seaport to the growing nation. The city adjusted to its losses. No. 29 Broadway, the rented mansion where the first family had lived, was turned into a hotel. Richmond Hill, the rented country estate on the Hudson just south of the village of Greenwich where Vice President Adams and his wife, Abigail, had stayed, acquired a new tenant, a thirty-four-year-old lawyer who had commanded a regiment during the war, named Aaron Burr.

In the Hudson River valley and north and west, the state was filling with New Englanders. Eastern Long Island had been largely settled by New Englanders, and Connecticut farmers had been drifting into Westchester, Dutchess, and Orange counties at a steady rate for a decade or more, but after 1783 the trickle became a torrent. The New Englanders poured in, traveling by ship, sleds, and oxcarts, many of them sweeping through the Mohawk gateway to settle down at least temporarily on the fertile plains of central and western New York. New York land speculators and developers were delighted. In one three-day period in February 1795, twelve hundred sleighs carrying New Englanders and their household possessions passed through Albany on the way to new farms in the Genesee country. The New England invasion more than made up for a temporary decline in immigration from Europe caused by the Napoleonic Wars. It also added a strong New England flavor to the attitudes of upstate New York.

Business and population alike boomed. The results of the first federal population census, taken in 1790, showed that New York City with 33,000 residents had passed Philadelphia as the biggest city in the United States. The city's population was not quite 10 percent of the population of the state. The import–export business was greatly improved by the horror of the wars in Europe, even though both France and Britain preyed upon the ships and trade that left New York harbor. In 1792, the value of exports from New York was about $2,500,000. In 1793, France declared war on Great Britain. Both countries clamored for goods and shipping, and the export business mushroomed—not all of it, of course, with the belligerents. By 1807, New York exports had increased 1000 percent, to $26,000,000. The city acquired a medical school in 1791—the College of Physicians and Surgeons, now part of Columbia University—and its first bank, the Bank of New York, in 1792, chartered at the urging of secretary of the treasury Alexander Hamilton. That same year, an out-of-doors meeting of brokers on Wall Street organized what is now the New York Stock Exchange.

Democracy spread rapidly in the state, but the great New York families retained much of the political influence they had enjoyed for most of the century. The resilient George Clinton had been elected governor for the fifth time in 1789, but by only a slim margin. His party, as before, controlled the New York Senate, but the Federalists won a majority of the seats in the Assembly.

One eventually tragic aspect of New York politics was the growth of rivalry between Alexander Hamilton and Aaron Burr. These two brilliant, ambitious men demonstrated an uncanny knack for getting in each other's way—perhaps because, in many ways, they were alike. Hamilton, in 1790, was thirty-three, a year younger than Burr. Burr was five feet six inches tall, Hamilton was five feet seven. They were both war veterans, noted for their straight, soldierly posture. They had both been academic prodigies. Burr, an orphan who had been raised by an uncle and whose father had been president of Princeton University, had been ready to enter at eleven, although the college made him wait until he was thirteen. Hamilton had come to New York from the West Indies, where he had had little formal schooling; nevertheless, King's College had been pleased to admit him as a special student at seventeen.

Burr's entry into politics came long after Hamilton's, and on the Anti-Federalist side. Governor Clinton had appointed Burr New York's attorney general in 1788, and Clinton backed Burr when he ran for the United States Senate in 1791. Burr won, defeating the man Hamilton was backing, the latter's father-in-law, Philip Schuyler. The Livingston family had turned away from Hamilton; they had originally favored his efforts to build the Federalist party in New York, but they were disenchanted by his failure as the first secretary of the treasury and dispenser of patronage to secure an important national post for any one of the Livingstons.

Thomas Jefferson feared that Hamilton's policies were schemes to exploit farmers, planters, and laborers for the benefit of capitalists, shipowners, and manufacturers. In the summer of 1791, Jefferson and Madison visited New York State and talked to Clinton, Robert R. Livingston, and Aaron Burr; and while no one knows exactly what was said, a political alliance among these Anti-Federalists (who were about to begin calling themselves Republicans, then Democratic–Republicans, and finally Democrats) seems to have been cemented.

In 1792, the Federalists hoped they could unseat Clinton by persuading John Jay to run against him. Jay was persuaded, even though he would have to step down from his post as Chief Justice of the United States if he won. The campaign was bitter. Clinton's canvassers, responsible for counting the ballots, won the election for Clinton by invalidating the Otsego, Tioga, and Clinton county votes on fragile technicalities. The next time around, in 1795, Jay was elected easily after Clinton—"The Old Incumbent," as his detractors called him—wisely decided not to run.

In the presidential election of 1796, after Washington had announced his decision against running for a third term, the campaigns were conducted for the first time on a fairly clear-cut Federalist-vs.-Republican party division. John Adams was the obvious Federalist candidate, with Thomas Pinckney of South Carolina as his running mate. Jefferson had in theory retired to Monticello, but the Republicans had no trouble nominating him as their best hope. The second man on the Republican ticket was more of a surprise: Aaron Burr. As the electoral college rules dictated, the candidate with the largest number of votes became president, and the man with the second largest number became the vice president, even if that meant that a Federalist president might serve with a Republican vice president, which is what happened. Adams won with 71 votes. Jefferson, with 68, was elected vice president. Burr got only 30 votes, but considering the short length of time that he had been in politics, it was rather remarkable that he was running at all.

Burr had worked hard for the Republicans (including himself). In 1797, his rising fortunes seemed stalled. His term in the Senate ended; with Jay as governor of New York and the Federalists in control of both houses of the New York legislature, it was evident that he would not be reelected. (The legislature chose Schuyler to take Burr's place.) But Burr was far from finished. He returned to New York City and the practice of law and ran for the New York Assembly in the fall of 1797, although his critics scoffed at what appeared to be a backward political step. In fact, Burr was looking ahead. Albany was an ideal place for him to cultivate more Republican support than he already had. Jefferson, frustrated as the Republican vice president in a Federalist administration, encouraged Burr to help him swing New York's strength to the Republican side. Burr was willing.

Compared to his rival, Hamilton, Burr's contribution to political thought and to the definition of the emerging United States had amounted to little—although, as minority leader in Albany, he initiated the proceedings that led to the gradual abolition of slavery in New York State. However, in the course of the next two years, Burr invented several political techniques, and improved on several old ones, that now seem completely up to date. Along the way, he recognized an enigmatic truth about the Federalists' support in the western frontier of New York State, the "Western District" as it was called. He saw that a good many of the frontier assemblymen who had been elected as Federalists and thought of themselves as Federalists—some of them had brought their Federalism with them from New

England—had unacknowledged Republican leanings. Burr concentrated on persuading a dozen of them—Obadiah German of Chenango County was one—to switch parties.

Since the Legislature chose New York's electors for the presidential election, Burr's diligence had tremendous leverage. State law required that the Legislature vote as a unit and choose either the Federalist or the Republican slate of twelve electors. Instead of being safely on the Federalist side, rural New York was fairly evenly divided, with a slight Republican tinge because of the changes in the Western District. The balance of power was in the counties on the lower Hudson valley, New York City, and the city's surrounding farm districts. They were the very heart of Federalist sentiment—in the previous election they had sent no Republicans to Albany.

Burr set about changing that situation starting in January 1800. It was taken for granted that the presidential race would be between the incumbent, Adams, for the Federalists and Jefferson for the Republicans. Burr hurried to Philadelphia to confer with Jefferson and obtain his assent to Burr's plans, and then he hurried back to New York City to build a vote-getting organization called the General Republican Committee, using his small band of personal followers, "the Burrites," as its nucleus. (By the next presidential election, Burr and the Burrites had made the Tammany Society, which met at Abraham Martling's tavern at the corner of Nassau and Spruce streets on the site of the first Tammany Hall, their political club; but as an organization, Tammany did not participate in Burr's General Republican Committee drive.) Burr had his men prepare a roster of every voter in the city, with a thumbnail dossier attached to each name: political preferences, temperament, willingness to serve the cause, and, most important, financial standing. Two-thirds of the city's free adult males, blacks included, were on the list, partly because both parties, from time to time, had used the device called "the tontine"—men who did not meet the property qualification banded together to purchase property jointly under a legal loophole that allowed each of them to claim the whole estate on election day. Burr sent groups of canvassers from door to door soliciting votes, volunteer help, and above all money. The General Republican Committee held exciting rallies in every neighborhood of every ward.

Perhaps Burr's greatest innovation was his all-star ticket of men to run for the Assembly, a slate he carefully kept secret until after Hamilton had announced the Federalist list of nearly unknown worthies: a banker, a ship chandler, a bookseller, and so on. Burr's slate was almost unbelievable. As Burr's biographer, Milton Lomask, has remarked, it read "like a page from the record book of the local peerage."[4] George Clinton, six times governor of the state, was at its head, followed by names like Horatio Gates, the hero of Saratoga; John Broome, president of the New York Insurance Company; Samuel Osgood, former postmaster general of the United States; and Brockholst Livingston of the Livingston clan. When the three days of balloting began on April 29, a flotilla of carriages, chairs, and wagons appeared to help Republican voters get to the polls. Burr dashed from one ward to the next, making speeches. The minute the polls closed, Burr's guards stationed themselves at every voting place to make sure that no inadvertent technical errors occurred. When the votes were counted, all thirteen of Burr's Republican candidates had been elected to the Assembly by a majority that averaged out to two hundred fifty votes per man. There was no doubt that Jefferson would have the votes of New York's twelve electors in the presidential contest.

With hindsight, Burr's brilliant organizational triumph can be seen as tragic. George Clinton or Robert Livingston might have been the Republicans' vice presidential candidate, instead of Burr. On the 11th of May, the Republicans met in caucus in Philadelphia and nominated Jefferson for the presidency and Burr for the vice presidency. When the votes were counted, Burr was tied with Jefferson, and the election again had to be decided by the House of Representatives, where each state had one vote. Hamilton used his influence with the Federalists to vote for Jefferson, not Burr: much as Hamilton disagreed with Jefferson, he had come to hate and fear Burr. Jefferson won by

4. Milton Lomask, *Aaron Burr* (New York: Farrar, Straus & Giroux, 1979), p. 241.

a single vote, and from then on, Jefferson and Clinton, worried by Burr's successes, froze Burr out of the top councils of the administration and of New York State. In 1804, when the time came for the next presidential election, Jefferson dropped Burr and chose Clinton to run with him as the vice presidential nominee.

Burr tried to run for the governorship of New York. Clinton's Democrats (as the Republicans were now calling themselves) refused to nominate their former organizational genius, and Burr was reduced to running as an independent. Hamilton worked hard for Burr's defeat. The Albany *Register* printed letters by a guest at a private dinner party who wrote that he had heard Hamilton call Burr a dangerous man and that in fact Hamilton had "a still more despicable" opinion of the man.

Burr's defeat for the governorship was crushing—the end, Burr felt, of his political career. On at least two earlier occasions, Burr had considered challenging Hamilton to a duel but had refrained from doing so. This time he sent his friend William Van Ness, a loyal Burrite, to Hamilton with the clippings of the Albany *Register* and a letter asking Hamilton "for an explanation." Hamilton did not want to duel, partly because his son, Philip, had been killed in a duel only three years earlier, and the shock had turned Hamilton against the widely popular practice—"the most barbarous of appeals," as Jefferson had called it. Hamilton was also unwilling to apologize. Nit-picking letters went back and forth, and in the end the duel was arranged for July 11, 1804.

Since dueling was illegal in New York, the New Yorkers' regular dueling ground was at Weehawken, across the Hudson in New Jersey. Nathaniel Pendleton, Hamilton's second, knew that Hamilton planned to demonstrate his courage by keeping the appointment and to show his disapproval of dueling by not firing. The men counted off the ten paces they had agreed on and loaded their pistols, and, in the few seconds after the command to fire, both pistols went off. The ball from Hamilton's gun went wide and snapped the branch of a tree twelve feet in the air. The ball from Burr's weapon hit Hamilton in the abdomen. The witnesses disagreed afterward about who fired first and whether Hamilton was firing at Burr. Hamilton's second and Dr. David Hosack, the New York physician who was present, took Hamilton to the home of Hamilton's friend William Bayard on Horatio Street in Greenwich Village. The next day, July 12, 1804, Hamilton died.

Hamilton had made many enemies during his life; he had been described as "a disgrace to the country" and a "menace to society." But his death inspired a wave of mourning. Flags were lowered, bells muffled, and entire editions of newspapers devoted to obituary accounts of his substantial accomplishments. No one forgave Burr. He was still the vice president of the United States—his term did not expire until March 1805—but he was ruined. Burr was astonished by the malice his fellow New Yorkers directed against him. For ten days he stayed at Richmond Hill, hoping that the tumult would subside. Then he learned that the coroner for the City and County of New York, with a fifteen-man jury, was investigating Hamilton's death. Burr assumed, correctly, that the coroner's jury would charge him with murder even though the duel had been fought in New Jersey. On July 21 the vice president fled to Philadelphia and on to St. Simons Island, off the coast of Georgia. His mind was beginning to fill with the assortment of megalomaniac land schemes that led to his trial (and acquittal) for treason in 1807.

The outrageous narrative story of Burr vs. Hamilton shows how great human potentialities can be squandered, yet there is a small, positive footnote. Today, when New York City is in pitifully short supply of eighteenth-century landmarks, history fanciers hold two in high regard: Hamilton's charming country house, The Grange, at Convent Avenue and 141st Street, which Hamilton left forever early on the morning of the duel; and the Jumel Mansion at 161st Street, overlooking the Harlem River valley, where Burr lived with his second wife, Madam Jumel, near the end of his long life. It had originally been the Roger Morris house, General Washington's headquarters during the battle for Manhattan. Both these houses are now museums, seemingly unaffected by the passionate ghosts who must hover around them.

10

The Western Connection

ＳOME time after Washington's inauguration and before the Civil War, an American style evolved—the most significant conclusion to the struggles for independence and nationhood. It was not definable, overall, in any brief descriptive phrase, and it was not by any means finished. However, in every field of endeavor, and in all institutions, and in manners, there came to be a distinctly American way of doing things so that any world traveller knew without having to inquire that he was not in England, France, or Germany, and certainly not in the Netherlands or China. New York's influences on this emerging national character were extraordinarily great.

Former Chancellor Robert R. Livingston, for instance, had a hand in the introduction of the steamboat to the Hudson River, and thus to all the rivers of the land. Livingston was appointed minister plenipotentiary to France in 1801, and there he scored a great diplomatic success by seizing the opportunity offered the United States to purchase Louisiana. He also met a tall, dark-haired Pennsylvanian, Robert Fulton, a portrait painter turned engineer who had been living in Europe for most of twenty years. Fulton had been born into a poor farm family forty-two years earlier and had shown remarkable talent as a boy for drawing. He had learned gunsmithing, and he drew the fanciful decorative designs that were much in demand by gunmakers. Fulton then had gone to Philadelphia to study art, and he had learned to paint portraits, miniatures, and landscapes. After he had saved enough money to buy his widowed mother a farm, he went to England. Four years later, in 1791, two of Fulton's paintings were included in the Royal Academy show. He traveled through England as he visited the country houses of people who had commissioned portraits, and he witnessed the changes that were taking place: new canals, new bridges, new machinery, and steam engines providing their power. He became acquainted with the Duke of Bridgewater and Lord Stanhope, and they encouraged him to devote all his time to engineering. Fulton patented machines for sawing marble, spinning flax, and twisting hemp rope and a "doubly inclined plane" for raising and lowering canal boats. In 1797, during a lull in the wars between England and France, Fulton went to Paris and built a remarkably successful submarine, *Nautilus,* which could submerge twenty-five feet, steered easily under water, and could stay submerged for more than four hours.

Livingston met Fulton in Paris, and they talked about steamboats. Livingston's brother-in-law, Colonel John Stevens of Hoboken, New Jersey, had been trying for some time to build a practical steamboat—inspired by the experiments of John Fitch and James Rumsey, who had launched steamboats with less than perfect success on the Delaware and Potomac rivers, respectively, in 1787. Livingston himself had found time to read every available paper on the subject. He had also secured the repeal of a New York State law of 1787 that had given Fitch sole rights to use steamboats on the Hudson, as well as the passage of an act giving that same privilege to himself, provided he could build a steamboat of twenty tons and propel it by steam at no less than four miles an hour. On October 10, 1802, Livingston and Fulton signed a legal agreement to construct a steamboat for the purpose of navigating the Hudson between New York and Albany. As George Dangerfield has remarked in his splendid biography of Livingston:

> What they had in mind, of course, was a revolution in national transport and economy. The country was rich in magnificent waterways—rivers, like the Mississippi, almost divine—down

which the populace and its produce floated to homestead or to market. But, in a sense, these were only semiwaterways; for neither populace nor produce could float up again. . . .[1]

An experimental boat financed by Livingston was built and launched on the Seine in 1803. Its machinery was too heavy, and it broke in two and sank. In the late summer of that year a new and stronger boat was tried and went well, making nearly three miles an hour. Before he left Europe, Fulton persuaded the English firm of Boulton & Watt to build an engine to his specifications and ship it to New York.

Work on the hull of the Livingston–Fulton steamboat started at the Charles Brown shipyard at Corlears Hook on the East River. In August 1807, *The Steamboat,* as it was then called, was ready to make its maiden voyage to Albany. Livingston had invited about forty guests, mostly relatives and close friends, to make the trip. Fulton got up steam with fuel of dry white pine. *The Steamboat* got under way and almost immediately stopped. In half an hour Fulton had the engine going again, and all those who had temporarily feared that the ship's nickname, "Fulton's Folly," had been justified were relieved.

The engine was noisy, and the splash of the side paddle-wheels was a sound that no one had heard before, but *The Steamboat* performed beautifully. The tale may not be true, but it is said that at the sight of the craft sailing through the night, with smoke and flame billowing from its chimney, a terrified farmer on shore rushed home, locked the door, and shouted that the Devil was on his way to Albany in a sawmill. At noon the following day, *The Steamboat* docked at the Clermont landing some ten miles above Rhinebeck, where the chancellor and some of the guests were to get off. Livingston held up his hand for silence, and happily announced the engagement of his second cousin once removed, Harriet Livingston, to Robert Fulton.

Fulton took the vessel on up the river to Albany and returned on August 21 to New York. The sailing time going up had been thirty-two hours; going down, thirty: a mean speed, Livingston

1. George Dangerfield, *Chancellor Robert R. Livingston of New York* (New York: Harcourt, Brace & Company, 1960), p. 405.

and Fulton calculated, of five miles an hour. By September 4, the partners were in business, carrying paying passengers from New York to Albany on a three-round-trips-a-week schedule. The fare, one way, was $7.

Meanwhile, the nation's long effort to remain neutral in the war between France and England was failing. That same year—1807—President Jefferson tried to isolate the United States from the conflict by getting Congress to pass the Embargo Act, which forbade United States ships to sail to any foreign port. Technically, importing was not forbidden; but few foreign ships were willing to call at United States ports because they were not allowed to sail away with anything in their holds except ballast. It was a mistaken policy, bitterly resented and resisted, nowhere more so than in New York. During Jefferson's last week in office, Congress finally abolished the Embargo Act and substituted the Non-Intercourse Act, which forbade trade only with Great Britain and France and authorized the president to end the boycott against either power by proclamation if it stopped violating the rights of neutrals.

The oncoming war between the United States and Great Britain had many causes, but none of them was more of an irritant as far as popular opinion in the United States was concerned than the royal navy's insistence that it had the right to stop any neutral ship upon the high seas and impress any British subject aboard into the service of the British navy. There were at least 10,000 British subjects working for American shipowners because working conditions in the American merchant marine, bad as they were, were better than in the British. When the royal navy stopped an American ship, however, the British officers seldom made a serious effort to distinguish between British subjects and Americans of English or Scottish descent. The exact figure will never be known, but between 1803 and 1812 at least 5,000 American sailors were impressed into the British Navy, and the number may have been twice as large.

In the agricultural west—the Ohio valley—frontiersmen were having trouble with Indians, and many of them believed that the British in Canada were responsible. Wheat, tobacco, and other agricultural prices were falling in the New Orleans markets, and westerners attributed that to British depredations. Numbers of frontiersmen took it for granted that the United States would take over Canada, if it came to war; and most likely Florida, too, since Spain had become Great Britain's ally. But only a few New Yorkers felt as enthusiastic about the prospects of war as a young generation in Congress—the "War Hawks," they were called—led by John C. Calhoun of South Carolina and Henry Clay of Kentucky.

In June of 1812 Congress declared war against Great Britain, less than a week before Lord Castlereagh, after a change of ministries, suspended the odious Orders in Council that had been the primary American grievance. England was suffering from a business depression, and British manufacturers, blaming many of their woes on their loss of United States markets, had been pressing for some sort of conciliation.

Much of the weight of the War of 1812, like the weight of the war for independence, fell on New York. The long border between Canada and the United States, especially the portion from Montreal to Detroit, appeared to be Great Britain's vulnerable front—there were no more than 2,500 British army regulars in place to defend the six-hundred-mile stretch, and among the War Hawks there were men who envisioned an easy, triumphant campaign. But the United States was quite unprepared to challenge the British navy. The United States fleet by now consisted of about a dozen first-class warships. Although they were faster, larger, and more powerfully armed than their British counterparts, they were too few. Despite some splendid victories in the first six months of the war, most of the American frigates were forced to spend most of the time at their moorings, unable to cope with the powerful British squadrons that patrolled the Atlantic coast.

United States privateers—merchant ships with cannons lashed to their decks—were more effective. There were several hundred of them, and they preyed on British shipping wherever they could find it. In the course of the two years' war, they captured more than 1,300 British ships. New York immediately contributed twenty-six privateers to the fleet and set to work building more. Within a year, however, the British moved in a blockading squadron that took up its station off Sandy Hook. There was then no way out of the harbor except through Hellgate, a treacherous passage, to Long Island Sound; a few months later, the British navy had control of the sound as well.

The strategy for the United States's invasion of Canada was complex—perhaps far too much so. Four separate, uncoordinated offensives were planned. The main army was to advance from Plattsburg, New York, up the old Lake Champlain invasion route to Montreal. The other three columns, mostly militiamen, were to attack from Detroit, Niagara, and Sacket's Harbor on Lake Ontario, just west of present-day Watertown. All the attacks failed. William Hull, the elderly governor of Michigan Territory, crossed the Detroit River into Canada and approached the British defenses but never attacked. Indians began to raid his line of supply, and Hull retired to Detroit. The British commander, Major General Sir Isaac Brock, followed and tricked Hull into surrendering Detroit. At Niagara, Major General Stephen van Rensselaer's advance guard made a surprise night crossing of the Niagara Gorge and established a strong toehold on the heights of Queenston. But the New York militia refused to follow, and the advance party was forced to surrender. About a month later, in November, Major General Henry Dearborn advanced twenty miles toward Montreal from Plattsburg, but when his column reached the Canadian border his militiamen refused to cross it. Dearborn marched them right back to Plattsburg. As for the planned attack from Sacket's Harbor, it did not materialize at all.

Given the unrealistic assumptions behind the American declaration of war, the collapse of President Madison's first offensive was not much of a surprise. Some of the fighting during the summer of 1813 was more profitable from the United States point of view. A 1,600-man army under Dearborn, with Commodore Isaac Chauncey's fleet providing transport and support, sailed from Oswego across Lake Ontario and burned the parliament buildings at the provincial capital, York (now Toronto). Then it sailed from Oswego to the mouth of the Niagara River and captured Fort George—a most skillful amphibious assault. In May, the Americans defended Sacket's Harbor against a British landing; and in July they repulsed a British raid on Black Rock near the mouth of the Niagara River. In September, Commodore Oliver Hazard Perry won a splendid victory over a British naval squadron at Put-in-Bay south of Detroit, which won control of Lake Erie for the United States. These were solid American victories, but they were not to be confused with a sweeping conquest of all Canada.

In July 1813, a British naval squadron took control of Lake Champlain, set fire to the barracks at Plattsburg, and stole some ammunition. As the year was coming to a close, the British forced the Americans out of Fort George; the retreating army put the torch to the villages of Queenston and Newark. The British responded by ravaging the American side of the Niagara, including Buffalo and Black Rock.

By the spring of 1814, after Napoleon's defeat, the British could shift large forces of seasoned troops to North America. The first element in the British plan was to send Sir George Prevost, with an 11,000-man army and a naval squadron, along Burgoyne's old route up Lake Champlain. It was hoped that the campaign would cut New England off from the other states and conceivably, given New England's intense disapproval of the war, tempt it to return to the British empire. The obstacles in Prevost's way were a 1,500-man force commanded by Brigadier General Alexander Macomb and a small fleet on Lake Champlain commanded by Commodore Thomas Macdonough. On September 11, the American sailors won a spectacular victory outside Plattsburg Bay. Prevost was afraid to advance without control of Lake Champlain. He turned around and went back to Canada.

The second element in the British offensive was a series of naval raids along the Atlantic coast. At the end of August 1814, Major General Robert Ross's British troops, escorted by Admiral Sir Alexander Cochrane's fleet, sailed into Chesapeake Bay and a considerable way up the Patuxent River and marched the remaining thirty miles to Washington, D.C. The capital's defense force was no match for the enemy. Ross's men burned most of the public buildings in Washington on August 24 and 25, and then withdrew with Baltimore as their next objective.

At the news of Washington's disaster, New York City turned with frenzy to building and repairing its defenses—Fort Jay on Governor's Island, Castle Clinton at the Battery, fortifications on Brooklyn Heights, Staten Island, Bedloe's Island, and Ellis Island, and a diagonal string of blockhouses across the middle of Manhattan—on the logical assumption that the British would be coming soon. But the lessons of history are not always perfectly clear. New Orleans, not New York, was the British objective after the failure of the naval bombardment of Fort McHenry at Baltimore, which left the Star Spangled Banner still there. Major General Andrew Jackson succeeded in defending New Orleans with great energy during the first two weeks in January, 1815—after the war was over, but before the news reached the combatants. Peace negotiations, which had dragged along since July, had been concluded on Christmas Eve. The British warship *Favorite* arrived at New York on February 11 with an account of the Treaty of Ghent; first the city, then the whole state rejoiced as the news was carried north and west.

Governor Daniel Tompkins proclaimed a day of public prayer, thanksgiving, and praise not long before the news came that Napoleon had escaped from Elba; but by the beginning of August, when New York heard about Waterloo, peace returned to a firm footing. Meanwhile privateers slipped into port, completing their final cruises; imports zoomed because Great Britain had picked New York, rather than any of the other United States ports, as the place to dump her accumulated stocks of export goods; and merchant ships began sailing for ports all over the world.

New York's rising star was the late vice president George Clinton's nephew, De Witt. He had been graduated from Columbia in 1786 and had studied law; he had served as his uncle's private secretary; then he had been elected to the New York Assembly, the New York Senate, and the United States

Senate. In 1803, he had resigned from the United States Senate to accept appointment as mayor of New York, and in that office he had done some excellent things. He was chief organizer of the Public School Society and the chief patron of the city's Orphan Asylum and the City Hospital. By 1812, Clinton was New York's lieutenant governor, filling a place left vacant by the death of John Broome. He had his eye on higher office.

In 1810, as mayor, Clinton had served on a state survey commission to study a route for a canal that might connect the Hudson River with Lake Erie. When peace returned, Clinton wrote an enthusiastic pamphlet describing the potential advantages of such a project. Along the 363-mile route there was great local enthusiasm for the idea, but the state legislature was uneasy about the cost. New York tried to get federal assistance; President Madison was not interested. By 1817, however, the president was James Monroe, and the vice president was Daniel D. Tompkins of New York. Clinton wanted to take Tompkins's place as governor. He rebounded from a deep sag in his political fortunes, partly because many of the New York voters identified him with the exciting "ditch" he had been advocating, and won the governorship with an extraordinary 95 percent of the popular vote.

Governor Clinton soon persuaded the legislature to authorize the canal, and he turned over the first ceremonial spadeful of earth at Rome on July 4. No other state had undertaken an engineering project on such a grand scale—neither had the nation, for that matter—and it took eight years to complete. At 10 o'clock on the morning of October 26, 1825, a canal barge, the *Seneca Chief,* left Buffalo bound for New York City via the Erie Canal. Governor Clinton and his wife were aboard. Guns boomed as the barge started; they had been stationed every few miles along the route, and each was fired as soon as the gunners heard the previous shot. Thus the signal that the governor had begun his trip reached New York City in an hour and a half. Clinton moved much more slowly. He stopped at Albany and other cities along the way for festive celebrations. A steamboat towed his barge down the Hudson, and on November 4, at

Sandy Hook, he stood on the prow of the *Seneca Chief* and poured a barrel of Lake Erie water into the Atlantic, celebrating "the wedding of the waters."

The canal had cost $9,000,000, but its value to New York and the nation was beyond reckoning. Freight that had cost $100 a ton to move now could be shipped for $6, and, with a way of getting their products to market, settlers poured into Indiana, Illinois, and Michigan. All along the canal new towns sprang up and old towns were charged with new vitality. Wheat grown in western New York, which had formerly been fed to pigs or distilled into whiskey because it was so expensive to move, could be shipped to seaboard markets for a few cents a bushel, as could Ohio wheat. Rochester quickly became the country's leading flour-milling center. Buffalo, a frontier outpost, began to grow into a major city. Tonawanda became the great transshipment point for Great Lakes states' lumber. At Albany, the hub of the canal trade, it was not unusual for fifty of the brightly painted canal boats, filled with passengers and cargo, to leave for the West in the course of a single day. New York now had a major link with expanding regions of the country.

11

Growing and Greening

$\mathcal{T}$HE population of New York State almost tripled between 1820 and 1860—from 1,370,000 to 3,880,000—and New York City steadily increased its lead as the nation's chief seaport. The introduction of scheduled transatlantic sailings of square-rigged packets, regardless of wind and weather, offered merchants dependable ways to ship their goods abroad. These first ocean liners, which averaged twenty-three days eastward to Liverpool and forty days on the return, started service in 1818. They were an immediate success. At the same time, New Yorkers developed coastal packet service to Charleston, Savannah, Mobile, and New Orleans, so that a major part of Southern cotton and produce went to Liverpool or Le Havre by way of Sandy Hook. This gave the eastbound packets a considerable part of their cargoes and filled New York businessmen's pockets with money.

No doubt New York City was also the Erie Canal's greatest beneficiary. Business on it far exceeded De Witt Clinton's most optimistic dreams by cutting freight costs as much as 90 percent. Total tonnage figures year after year set new records, reaching a peak in 1872 of 6,000,000 tons. Towns that were not close to the Erie naturally aspired to canals of their own, and an expensive network of feeder canals and waterway connections was built—in a good many cases, quite unjustifiably from a balance-sheet standpoint. The Hudson itself was getting crowded. By 1850 more than one hundred steamers were carrying more than a million passengers a year, and the fastest of the boats—which had become wonderfully elegant—could make the New York-to-Albany run in less than eight hours.

In the midst of the state's waterway extravaganza, a specimen of the next era of steam rattled over iron-capped wooden rails from Albany to Schenectady: the first train on New York's first railroad, the Mohawk and Hudson, open for business in August 1831. The earliest railroad lines were short, from a marketplace out into the nearby countryside; but connections were made, the gaps between clusters were filled, and by 1842 one could board a train at Buffalo and ride all the way to Albany. The Erie Railroad, which ran from Piermont to Dunkirk on Lake Erie across the southern tier of New York, was complete by 1851—for the moment the longest continuous line in the world. New York City for once was laggard about understanding what a new means of transportation would mean to the city, the state, and the country; New York City financiers could not get their minds off steamboats. The Hudson River Railroad from New York City was not finished as far as Albany until 1851—and then the station was in *East* Albany, the wrong side of the river. (Rensselaer, the Albany stop for Amtrak trains from New York City today, is also on the wrong side of the river. But railroading is not what it was.) By 1853, Erastus Corning, an Albany merchant, had consolidated eight short lines into another transstate system, the New York Central. By 1860 almost all of the heavily populated sections of the state, even Long Island, had railroad service.

Thanks to the canal and the railroads, Albany was the center of the United States wholesale lumber trade by 1840, and the city remained a major lumber center for decades thereafter. As early as 1813 rafts of logs were floated to mills at Glens Falls from the Adirondacks, and completion of the canal meant that lumber from Michigan and Ohio could be shipped through Tonawanda and on to Albany economically. By 1865 there were almost 4,000 lumber mills in the state, and in the last half of the nineteenth century nearly five billion board feet of sawn lumber were produced.

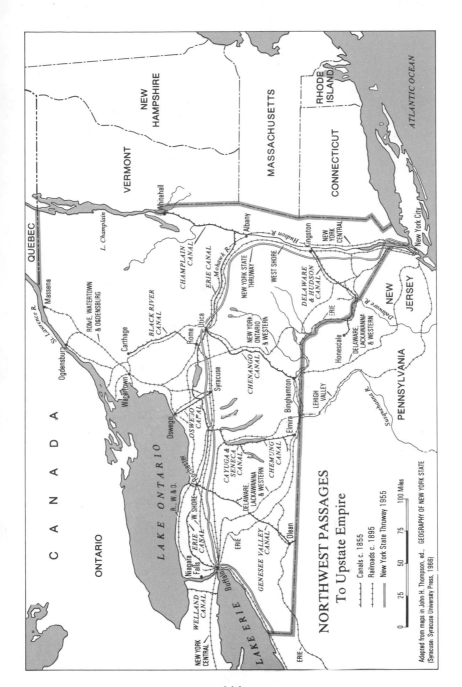

NORTHWEST PASSAGES
To Upstate Empire

Canals c. 1855
Railroads c. 1895
New York State Thruway 1955

0   25   50   75   100 Miles

Adapted from maps in John H. Thompson, ed., GEOGRAPHY OF NEW YORK STATE
(Syracuse: Syracuse University Press, 1966)

New York State's massive lumber industry literally made possible the building of New York City—and helped build more than one substantial fortune. When John Jacob Astor died in 1848 he left a fortune of $20,000,000, more money than any American had ever made before—and Astor had suffered heavy losses during the War of 1812, when the British took possession of his central fur depot, Astoria, at the mouth of the Columbia River. Born in Germany, Astor had come to New York City immediately after the end of the Revolutionary War and had made his first fortune in the fur trade by trading much farther west than most—in Canada, around the western Great Lakes, and as far as the Pacific. His second fortune was made in shipping. By 1803, Astor was trading as far as China in his own ships. His third fortune was made in New York City real estate, and Astor's strategy was simple: he bought, but he never sold. He bought well beyond the city's limits in some cases, confident that the pattern of growth would continue. He bought the Eden Farm, for instance, which is now Times Square, from Forty-second to Forty-sixth Street.

Astor seldom built on his land himself. He leased it for quite a long time, often twenty-one years; when the lease expired, he raised the rent or, if the new figure horrified the tenant, he bought the tenant's building at an advantageous price. He came to own a lot of tenements, because the builders who leased land could make more money out of tenements than anything else. Astor's investments in real estate were estimated at $2,000,000. By the time he died, the properties were worth a sizable part of the $20,000,000. By 1900, their value was close to $450,000,000. One of Astor's critics, James Gordon Bennett, denounced him in the *New York Herald* as a "self-invented money making machine" and argued that half of Astor's fortune belonged by rights to the people of New York. Bennett meant that the city, by cutting up Manhattan into rectangular blocks, had transformed acres of common lands, farms, and country estates into the world's most valuable real estate and that Astor had not had to *do* anything to reap the benefits. Since that was exactly why Astor had invested as he had, Bennett's outrage was a little tardy.

Astor did return something. He left no money to charities, but he set up a $400,000 fund to endow a library—the Astor Library—which was opened in 1854 on LaFayette Street. It soon contained 100,000 volumes, and it was at the time the finest reference library in the United States. It later combined with the Lenox and Tilden foundations. In 1911 they opened the great building at Forty-first Street and Fifth Avenue, on the site of the old Bryant Park Reservoir—The Public Library, as all New Yorkers call it. It is a private library operated for the public's benefit.

The invasion of New Englanders had by no means ended, but New York was also called upon to make room for a great many newcomers from more distant lands. After the Russians had put down the Polish revolution of 1830, the state became a refuge for a good many Poles. Potato famine sent over southern Irish by the million between 1840 and 1860; the revolutions of 1848 sent a flood of Germans to the port of New York. Tens of thousands of the European immigrants continued on, up the Hudson and west, some of them as far as the Ohio and the Mississippi and even farther. In 1831, when Alexis de Tocqueville and Gustave de Beaumont explored America, travelling 4,000 miles and seeing something of all twenty-four of the states, Michigan Territory was the edge of the frontier. De Tocqueville was surprised that the pioneers in the wilderness closely resembled the men he had seen in the cities: "The man you left in New York you find again in almost impenetrable solitudes: same clothes, same attitude, same language, same pleasures." The explanation, he understood, was that the frontiersmen had arrived only "since yesterday." [1]

The old New York families of Dutch and English descent were being nudged out of power in state politics and replaced by New Englanders. From 1821 to 1836, Albany was dominated by the "Albany Regency": Democrats under the leadership of Martin Van Buren, first and foremost, and others including

---

1. Quoted in John A. Garraty, *The American Nation: A History of the United States* (New York: Harper & Row, 1966), p. 288.

Silas Wright, William Learned Marcy, Azariah Cutting Flagg, and John A. Dix. The Albany Regency was an offshoot of Tammany, and it was opposed vigorously by the Whigs and later the Republican party under the leadership of Thurlow Weed, William H. Seward, Hamilton Fish, and Horace Greeley. Every one of these dominant New York figures, with the exception of Van Buren, was either a native New Englander or of New England descent.

By 1850, there were 134,000 Irish-born residents of New York City, 26 percent of the population. Some of the Irish, to be sure, had ancestors who had arrived during the seventeenth and eighteenth centuries; some, like Thomas Addis Emmet, the state's attorney general in 1812, had achieved high public office. By the time of the great migration a sizable Irish Catholic community was established in New York City, and the Irish vote counted heavily. After the great migration, and for perhaps fifty years, it practically *was* the New York City vote: the Irish seemed to take over the city's political system and transform it into something rather like an enlarged version of an Irish village's social structure.

The Irish village was a place where everyone had a role to play under the watchful eye of a stern oligarchy of elders. Starting from ward committees, Tammany established an efficient hierarchy, with the building captain at the bottom, leading up to the block captain, the district captain, and the county leader. Every position on the organizational chart had definite rights and responsibilities that had to be observed. After consolidation of the five boroughs into New York City, an assembly of all the county committees came to 32,000 persons—a bureaucracy that needed to hire Madison Square Garden for a meeting, assuming that only half the eligibles would attend. The efficiency of that bureaucracy in getting out the Democratic vote on election day was formidable.

In 1850, New York City—unable to see the Irish cast of things to come—was inhospitable. The immigrants were swindled unmercifully from the moment they stepped off the boat, having already been robbed in many cases by the shipowners who had brought them across the Atlantic. The city tried to "bond" the immigrants, creating a breed of professional bondsmen–racketeers. In the boarding houses that catered to the new arrivals, they were sold fake steamboat and railroad tickets and charged exorbitant rents for space that hardly fitted any definition of "rooms." By one count, 18,000 New Yorkers—mostly the immigrants—in New York City were living in cellars. Nevertheless, every ship that docked at New York added to the stream of new arrivals, until by 1860 some 300,000 people were living in the city's slums. Of those, 200,000 had arrived—or at least their parents had arrived—after 1845, mixing the New Irish and Germans with the poor New Yorkers who had lived there for a longer time. Every part of New York State received some immigrants. The census of 1855 showed that 30,000 of Buffalo's 79,000 population were German-speaking and that 44 percent of the population of Rochester was foreign-born, with Germany the main country of origin.

Even though the demand for unskilled labor—and for skilled labor, too—was tremendous, the *New York Tribune* had estimated a few years earlier that New York City's slum-dwellers were living on $1 a week on average. Hotels, boarding houses, and the town houses of the New York City rich employed an army of servants who were content with wages of $6 a month, plus board and lodging; and housekeepers and chambermaids, cooks and waiters, were well off compared to needleworkers who sewed garments at home. A few trade unions had been organized, with the printers and the shoemakers leading the way, but the financial panic of 1837, the depression of 1854–1855, and the panic of 1857 had dampened their efforts to improve working conditions.

The pressures for more living space were strong. The average urban dweller throughout the state expected to walk to work. There were a few horsecar lines on Manhattan, and a number of omnibuses, but the traffic was very heavy. New York City's rich, who could afford to keep horses and carriages, built their new town houses farther and farther and farther uptown. By 1860, the elegant expansion had passed Washington Square and was headed north, up Fifth Avenue, toward Madison Square at Twenty-third Street.

The 1807–1811 gridiron plan for the city's future expansion had not provided for a really big park (nor had it dreamed of the possibility that the island might fill up with buildings north of 155th Street). As early 1844, William Cullen Bryant had proposed such a park; the problem was where to put it, since hardly anyone could oppose a park on principle. In 1851 Andrew Jackson Downing, who at the age of thirty-six had become the outstanding landscape architect in the United States, published an article in the magazine he edited, the *Horticulturist,* suggesting that the park ought to be where in fact it is—between 59th and 110th streets and between Fifth and Eighth avenues. The City Council, persuaded, asked the Legislature for permission to buy the land, which was divided into several thousand lots owned by many different people. Central Park's land—840 acres—cost more than $5,000,000: a bargain nonetheless, as by 1853 there were only 117 acres of true open space left in the city.

In 1857, the Park Commissioners held a competition with a prize of $2,000 for the best park plan. The winning design was the work of two men, Frederick Law Olmsted and Calvert Vaux. Olmsted, who was in his thirties, was working as the park superintendent—although site superintendent might have been a more accurate title. Vaux was an English-born architect who had worked with Downing and had landscaped parts of Washington, D.C. Their concept was to redesign nature to make it more beautiful and, if possible, more natural.

Olmsted had been supervising the preparation of the place, which meant evicting five thousand squatters living in shanties who had not wanted to go (neither had their pigs and goats). The park's streams were sewers, the swamps were garbage dumps. The pair filled in an old receiving reservoir and built a new one north of Eighty-sixth Street; the path around it is now a favorite track for midtown joggers. They saved an old 1812 stone fort near the northwest corner of the park and the state militia arsenal at Sixty-fifth Street and Fifth Avenue, now the Park Department's headquarters. And they transformed the heart of the island into an inspired vision of what Nature, with assistance, can be. Central Park, as V. S. Pritchett has expressed it, gave New York City "the lovely and long green main deck" and "a focus or a style, and in the carriage days, a meeting place."[2] New Yorkers took Central Park to their hearts long before its completion. For many residents, it was a reachable or closer-to-home version of the increasingly popular resort areas in the Catskills and Adirondacks. They skated on its ponds, they rowed on its lakes, they showed off their best carriages on its winding roads.

Olmsted and Vaux went on to plan Prospect Park in Brooklyn as well as Riverside and Morningside parks in Manhattan. Olmsted led the move to make Yosemite a state reservation and made designs for the suburban development at Riverside, near Chicago. The two men set up a firm in 1865, and for thirty years they executed an amazingly far-flung business designing city parks, planning cities, landscaping private estates and historic sites, and designing university campuses: the Boston park system, with its famous Arnold Arboretum; Chicago's South Park, Detroit's Belle Isle Park, Montreal's Mount Royal Park, and many more. They designed the Capitol grounds at Washington, D.C., and at Albany, New York; they helped plan Stanford University; and in 1893 they designed the grounds of the "White City" for the Chicago World's Fair. In terms of impact on American style, Olmsted and Vaux achieved some sort of record. Not every city in the United States employed the firm; but whenever a group of city fathers saw Central Park after the Civil War, they aspired to something of the sort—provided that space could be found—for their home town.

Olmsted's influence is found in New York State outside urban boundaries too. He was instrumental in obtaining public support for the Niagara Reservation, a tourist attraction for nearly a century before its dedication in 1885 as the second state park in the nation (after Yosemite). In that same year, when the Adirondack Forest Preserve was established, Olmsted's magazine *Garden and Forest* argued persuasively and successfully against allowing leaseholds on public lands within the reserve.

The Adirondack Park is unique. Not only is it the largest park

2. V. S. Pritchett, *New York Proclaimed* (New York: Harcourt, Brace & World, 1965), p. 45.

in the country—some six million acres, of which 38 percent is public land and 62 percent in private hands—but the state holdings are protected by constitutional provisions against any change without a statewide referendum. The park's origins go back to the dreams of De Witt Clinton, who wanted the watershed preserved partly to maintain the Erie Canal.

12

Portraits of Ourselves

EW York drew ahead of its fellow states in other ways, less obviously connected with transportation and commercial and urban foresight. It became a center for people—some natives, some not—interested in literature, journalism, painting, and the other arts. Washington Irving, a native New Yorker, was the city's first professional author. His brother, Peter, owned the *New York Morning Chronicle,* and Washington's first pieces ("The Letters of Jonathan Oldstyle") appeared in its pages. Irving's comic *History of New York,* allegedly by Diedrich Knickerbocker, was published in 1809, and his *Sketchbook,* which contained both "Rip van Winkle" and "The Legend of Sleepy Hollow," appeared in New York and London in 1819 and 1820.

James Fenimore Cooper, the most famous novelist of his day, grew up in Cooperstown, attended Yale, and was commissioned as a Navy midshipman in 1807. After his marriage to Susan De Lancey, he lived at Mamaroneck and later Scarsdale. His second novel, *The Spy* (1821), a romantic suspense story set in the American Revolution, is said to have been based in part on recollections Cooper had heard from his Westchester neighbor John Jay. It was a considerable success. In 1822 Cooper went to New York City, and in the following year he published both *The Pioneers*—which introduced the marvelous character Natty Bumppo—and *The Pilot. The Last of the Mohicans* appeared in 1826.

After a stay of several years in Europe, Cooper returned to the United States to realize—to his own dismay—that the ideal wilderness of his imagination and the simple, virtuous, enlightened patriotism of Americans were not exactly as he had depicted them. He was angry at his fellow countrymen for their attacks on his attempts to contrast European and American principles, and he temporarily retired as a novelist in his *Letter to His Countrymen,* published in 1834. No matter the attacks and his own disillusionment; with Irving, Cooper had provided the world and New York State especially with *improved* history—funnier, more exciting, far more memorable than the stubborn facts the historians would struggle to assemble.

William Cullen Bryant, a lawyer born and raised in Massachusetts, became one of New York's most famous newspaper editors although he must have considered himself at heart a nature poet. He practiced law in Massachusetts for ten years, from 1815 to 1825; but he had written "Thanatopsis" in 1811 (it did not appear until 1817, when *The North American Review* ran an abbreviated version in its September issue), and lyrics like "Green River," "To A Waterfowl," and "Forest Hymn" before he changed professions. He moved to New York and got a job as an assistant editor of the *Evening Post* in 1826, with the intention of using journalism to pay his bills while he devoted himself to literature. Bryant became editor of the *Evening Post* in 1829, and he ran it until he died in 1878. The paper had been founded by Alexander Hamilton in 1801 to support the Federalists; under Bryant's editorship it spoke for the Democrats until 1848, when the paper broke with the party to champion Martin Van Buren's Free-Soil candidacy. By 1853, the *Evening Post* had taken a strong anti-slavery stand. Bryant introduced Abraham Lincoln at Cooper Union in 1860 and supported Lincoln in 1864, while scolding him for his hesitation in proclaiming full emancipation of the slaves. The paper remained Republican, despite the Ulysses S. Grant administration, until the day Bryant died. Somehow he saved enough creative energy to produce and publish new poems from time to time. His last poetic work was a blank-verse translation of Homer, which was completed in 1872.

Horace Greeley came to New York City from East Poultney, Vermont, where he had learned the printer's trade. He opened a printing shop with a partner in 1833, did some writing on the side for Whig newspapers, and founded an unsuccessful literary and news weekly called the *New Yorker*. Greeley boarded with a temperance lecturer from Connecticut named Sylvester Graham, who advocated coarsely ground whole-wheat flour—it came to be known as Graham flour, suitable for crackers—loose, light clothing, daily exercise, fresh vegetables, fresh fruits, hard mattresses, and pure drinking water. Greeley thought quite a lot of Graham's radical enthusiasms, but many New Yorkers considered them funny—especially after Ralph Waldo Emerson called Graham "the poet of bran bread and pumpkins"—and after 1840 not many people listened to Graham's advice.

In 1841, Greeley founded his *New York Tribune,* a Whig penny paper, and within five years it was widely considered the city's best: distinguished for its excellent reporting, its high moral standards, and its vigorous, fair-minded editorials. Until after the Civil War, the *Tribune*'s political influence was very great. Greeley's own earnestness, his enthusiasm for reforms of all kinds, and his deft way with a phrase ("Go West, young man") gave the *Tribune* and its editor direct, personal appeal that journalism had not known before.

With television the main source of news for most Americans, the crucial role of newspapers, dating from before the Revolution, may seem implausible; but at the middle of the nineteenth century, newspapers and magazines were everything, except for word of mouth. Men like Bryant and Greeley were helping invent the newspaper, setting standards, establishing style; their influence, along with the influences of a great many other New York editors, reached into the editorial offices of every newspaper in the country.

Hundreds of other writers moved to New York. Edgar Allan Poe came from Philadelphia in 1844, bringing his young wife, Virginia, with him, and they lived in a cottage in Fordham, now part of the Bronx. Less than a year later "The Raven" appeared in the *New York Evening Mirror,* and Poe published both his

Tales and *The Raven and Other Poems* in 1845. Lorenzo da Ponte, Italian poet and author of the librettos for three of Mozart's operas—*Le Nozze di Figaro, Don Giovanni,* and *Cosi Fan Tutte*—came to New York in 1805 at the urging of Clement Clarke Moore, Hebrew scholar and poet and principal benefactor of New York's General Theological Seminary. (Moore is likely never to be forgotten on account of his ballad, "A Visit From St. Nicholas," which was first published in the Troy, New York, *Sentinel,* and begins: " 'Twas the night before Christmas, when all through the house. . . .") Da Ponte became the first professor of Italian literature at Columbia and taught numbers of New Yorkers to appreciate the poetry of Dante. The city was not quite ready for an opera company of its own, but da Ponte welcomed the opera star Manuel Garcia when he and his family troupe of singers visited New York. Their performances of *Il Barbiere di Siviglia* and *Don Giovanni* at the Park Theater during the 1825–1826 season were the first operas New York had heard sung in Italian.

Walt Whitman, born in 1819 at Huntington, Long Island, grew up in Brooklyn. He started to learn printing at thirteen as an apprentice at the *Long Island Patriot* and worked for nine or ten different papers before he was thirty, occasionally contributing pieces to them. He edited the *Brooklyn Eagle* for two years, published a temperance novel, explored the city, rode the ferries and buses, went to the theater whenever he could, and loved opera. There was practically no hint in the few poems and melodramatic stories he had published before 1855 that Whitman was a great poet. But that year, when the first edition of *Leaves of Grass* appeared, a few people immediately responded to Whitman's work—led by Emerson, who thanked him for a copy with a letter that included: "I greet you at the beginning of a great career." *Leaves of Grass* was a popular failure—it was regarded as scandalous, or unintelligible, or a little of both—but Whitman nursed it through twelve editions, adding, revising, and rearranging its contents. Sales were invariably disappointing, but the poet's admirers and imitators grew steadily—a process that has not yet stopped. Emerson's enthusiasm could not have been more accurate.

New York City native Herman Melville, a grandson of Peter Gansevoort, the defender of Fort Stanwix, grew up in Albany, worked as a bank clerk, a shopkeeper, a farmhand, a school-teacher, and at eighteen as a cabin boy on the New York–Liverpool run. At twenty-two he shipped out of Fairhaven, Massachusetts, aboard the whaler *Acushnet;* deserted ship in the Marquesas Islands a year and a half later; lived for a month in the Typee valley; worked as a field hand in Tahiti; enlisted in the United States Navy; and returned to Boston in 1844. He knew what he was going to write about and began immediately. *Typee* (1846) and *Omoo* (1847) promptly made Melville famous. He married Elizabeth Shaw, daughter of the chief justice of Massachusetts, and they moved to New York in 1847. By 1851, Melville had written four more novels: *Mardi, Redburn, White-Jacket,* and *Moby Dick.* His next book, *Pierre,* published the following year, was autobiographical; and some readers realized that there had been more strain and greater disappointments concealed by Melville's dazzling literary triumphs than the world imagined.

The critics did not appreciate *Moby Dick,* and its sales were disappointing; in 1853, a fire destroyed the plates and stacks of unsold copies. Melville tried to get a consulship without having any luck; he took to lecturing to make some money; he wrote some poetry. *Israel Potter,* a novel about the Revolutionary War published in 1855, was a good book—but not in a class with *Moby Dick.* Melville withdrew almost completely from society and the literary world. In 1866, he got a steady job as a customs inspector in New York City and worked at it for twenty years. Not long before he died in 1891, he completed the manuscript of his extraordinary short novel, *Billy Budd.* But he was almost completely forgotten. As his obituary in the *New York Press* remarked: "Probably, if the truth were known, even his own generation had long thought him dead, so quiet have been the later years of his life." Melville's real importance was not perceived until the 1920s. His first biography appeared in 1921. *Billy Budd* was finally published in 1924. *Moby Dick,* in new editions, reconsidered by critics all over the world, began to contend for the title of greatest of the great American novels.

There had been professional painters, mostly portrait painters, in New York since Dutch days. The five or six men who painted portraits of New Yorkers of Dutch descent between 1715 and 1730 constitute the first clearly recognizable school in American art—the "Patroon Painters," as James T. Flexner calls them. After the War of 1812, and especially after 1825, American painting broke loose from its European moorings. Before it did, nearly all of the country's best painters had studied in Europe, and a remarkable group—John Trumbull, Charles W. Peale, Gilbert Stuart, Robert Fulton, Thomas Sully, Samuel F. B. Morse, and Charles R. Leslie, among others—had studied with Benjamin West, a Pennsylvania-born, Quaker-bred former sign painter who had been a charter member of the Royal Academy and its president after 1792, succeeding Sir Joshua Reynolds. (King George III, who was not overly fond of all Americans, liked West and admired his painting and appointed him his official historical painter.)

In 1822 a young immigrant from Lancashire, England's textile-manufacturing center, who had persuaded his father to move his family to the United States in 1818, set out from Steubenville, Ohio, as an itinerant portrait painter. His name was Thomas Cole, and he was twenty-one years old. He had had no training. In the course of his meanderings, Cole learned that he did not like portrait painting. His preference was landscapes—an inferior branch of the art in the view of the world's connoisseurs.

In 1825, a New York City frame maker displayed three Hudson River landscapes for sale in the window of his shop. They were by Thomas Cole, who had learned a good deal in the interval by studying the pictures in Philadelphia's art galleries and at the Pennsylvania Academy of Art, and by making sketches only a few months earlier of the Catskills. Colonel John Trumbull, New York's best-known painter, happened to notice them. Trumbull was an old man at sixty-nine, the first major artist to set up a studio in New York, and renowned as "the painter of the Revolution"—"The Battle of Bunker Hill," "Death of General Montgomery in the Attack on Quebec," "Surrender of Lord Cornwallis at Yorktown," "Declaration of Independence," those vast, detailed, historical concoctions that have been reproduced in every American history book ever since and are our image of the way it should have looked. Trumbull was overwhelmed by Cole's exuberant, powerful landscapes. He saw "the American land depicted in all its native peculiarity with powerful realism and yet a lover's eye." Trumbull hurried to William Dunlap's studio to announce his discovery: "This young man," Trumbull said, "has done what all my life I attempted in vain to do."[1]

Without the slightest notion that he was doing so, Cole had founded the first major school of American painting, the "Hudson River School." It was made up of a diverse group of men who influenced each other, approached landscape painting in similar ways, but were also strongly individual in their aims and achievements. Their portraits of the state's hills, lakes, valleys, waterfalls, and rivers are a magnificent record of New York at the time. Next to Cole as leader in the Hudson River School was Asher B. Durand, and there were many others—Thomas Doughty and Alvin Fisher (who had both started painting pure landscape before Cole), John Frederick Kensett, Frederick E. Church, Albert Bierstadt, Jasper Francis Cropsey, and Thomas Moran. In general they shared a view that painting was primarily the representation of the external world, and that they could express their love of nature by meticulous accuracy in every detail. Some of them—Church, Bierstadt, and Moran, for instance—went on beyond the wonders of New York to paint the Rockies, Yosemite, the Grand Canyon, and even the snow-capped peaks of the Andes.

The popular response to Cole's work was splendid. For two generations or more ordinary New Yorkers bought Hudson River School pictures and other realistic depictions of what was undeniably there to be caught on canvas, like William Sidney Mount's genre paintings of Long Island farm life. The flat potato fields, the dunes, the brilliant light, the beguiling influence of the sea and salt spray upon landscape, drew many artists to

---

1. Quoted in James T. Flexner, *History of American Painting,* Vol. 3, *That Wilder Image* (New York: Dover Books, 1970), p. 5.

the eastern end of Long Island. The Hamptons influenced their
perceptions and imaginations much as the Hudson River and the
Catskills had acted upon Cole and Durand, although in such a
variety of ways, and on men and women of such a variety of
styles and concepts, that they cannot be considered a school of
Long Island painters. Thomas Moran, already famous for his
western mountain scenes, built an impressive studio on East
Hampton's main street facing the village green and pond and
made it his home. Moran was born in England and brought to
the United States when he was seven. He was trained as a
young man as a wood engraver and illustrator. In 1852, when
he was twenty-five years old, Moran visited England and was
inspired by the work of J. M. W. Turner, who had died just a
year earlier. Moran balked at the idea of painting subjects or
scenes that Turner might have used. "I will paint as an American on an American basis," Moran said, and he returned to the
United States.

He soon discovered that finding an American landscape on
which he could employ Turneresque techniques was not the easiest thing in the world; but in 1870 *Scribner's Magazine* needed
a picture of the Grand Canyon of the Yellowstone to illustrate
an article. The editors asked Moran to do the illustration.
Moran's problem was that he had never seen the Yellowstone,
and he imagined that it was narrow. The following year, he saw
his subject. His vast oil, "Grand Canyon of the Yellowstone"—fifteen feet wide and eight feet tall, with Turneresque
mist rising above the falls—and a companion painting, "Chasm
of The Colorado," were bought by the Congress of the United
States for $10,000 apiece. They were the first adequate pictorial
records of the scenery of those natural wonders, and in 1872
Congress established Yellowstone National Park "as a pleasur-
ing ground for the benefit and enjoyment of the people." It was
the first of the nation's system of national parks, and Moran's
spectacular canvas, showing the canyon's proper width, swung
a good many of the legislators' votes to the affirmative side.

A complete catalogue of the distinguished artists who have
worked at the eastern end of Long Island would be very long.
Winslow Homer, who visited East Hampton in the early 1870s,

was one of the first to respond to the landscape's pictorial possibilities. The list would also include the sculptor Augustus Saint-Gaudens, born in Ireland and raised in New York City, whose marble "Hiawatha" at Saratoga, New York, and equestrian statue of General William T. Sherman at the southeast corner of Central Park in New York City, among many other works, are world famous; and Childe Hassam, one of America's foremost Impressionists, who died in East Hampton in 1935. In 1891, William Merritt Chase, a president of the Society of American Artists, founded the Shinnecock Summer School of Art in Southampton. For eleven summers Chase sent hundreds of pupils, including Howard Chandler Christy and Joseph Stella, scrambling across the dunes and through the moors of the Shinnecock Hills learning to paint directly and out of doors. Chase was a fine painter as well as a prodigious teacher. He was convinced that a canvas should be finished quickly, on the scene; the danger in making sketches and taking them back to the studio, and laboring over the painting, is that the true impact of the landscape on the artist's sense may be forever lost.

The landscape painting that Doughty, Cole, Durand, and their many successors produced was a vital and valid expression of the way the nation felt about itself; and the leading American collectors bought American pictures. The fact that, for most of the twentieth century, this native work was underrated and neglected by art sophisticates had its compensations; the last laugh belongs to those whose grandfathers loved Church and Kensett on sight, bought their pictures, and kept them in reasonably good repair. People who could not afford an original Moran loved the countless polychromatic reproductions of his western scenery as they appeared on thousands of calendars. And as early as the middle of the nineteenth century a good American painter was at least as likely to be able to support himself and his family by painting as he was a century or a century and a quarter later.

While the New York landscapes were inspiring native American art, the state was alive with religious fervor of great variety. Many of the settlers who moved into upstate (and especially western) New York from New England brought strong religious convictions with them. Often whole communities moved together, most from the New England hill country and most of them disciples of Jonathan Edwards: no Halfway Covenanters these. They tended to believe in the perfectibility of mankind and in millenialism, and a great many of the more notable (and eccentric) nineteenth-century religious movements began or developed in the region. It has become known as the "Burned-over District" because of the quantity of fiery revival movements that swept repeatedly across it especially between 1825 and 1860. The region is a marked contrast to adjacent western Pennsylvania—settled from the South rather than the Northeast.

Revivalist meetings, calling on the members of the congregation to convert from a state of sin to a state of grace, were popular long before 1825. But in that year Charles Grandison Finney, a handsome man and an inspiring orator who had just been ordained a Presbyterian minister, led a revival at Western, a small town not far from Rome. He was so successful there that Rome, Utica, and Rochester beseeched him to visit their churches and do for them what he had done for Western. Finney did move to Rochester in 1830 and converted thousands in one of the most successful revivals of all time.

Also in 1830, Joseph Smith founded the Church of Jesus Christ of Latter-day Saints at Fayette, a few months after he had published the Book of Mormon. Smith, a native of Vermont, lived in Palmyra, and it was there between 1820 and 1823 that he experienced a series of visions which led him to believe that God had selected him to restore the church of Christ. He reported that on a hill not far from his home he had found gold plates on which the story of the true church was engraved. His miracles and prophecies interested quite a few of his neighbors, but the original group of about 100 Mormons moved on to Kirtland, Ohio, in 1831. Later, oppressed wherever they tried to settle, they went on to Illinois (where Joseph Smith was murdered), Missouri, and then their own Zion of Utah. Returning Mormon missionaries converted other residents of the Burned-over District in the 1830s and 1840s, and the Church of Jesus

Christ of Latter-day Saints is undeniably one product of the region's religious fervor that prospered and grew.

John Humphrey Noyes, born in Brattleboro, Vermont, and a product of Dartmouth and the Andover and Yale theological schools, found a firmer footing on New York soil than had Joseph Smith. Noyes, like Finney, reacted against Calvinism and, having persuaded himself that he had attained a state of perfection, formed a society in Putney, Vermont, known as the "Bible Communists." Noyes's doctrines for successful communal living included "promiscuity" within the group, and that led to his arrest on a charge of adultery. In 1848, having jumped bail, Noyes fled to Oneida in central New York and established the Oneida Community—perhaps the most successful in a material sense of the multitude of American utopian experiments.

There were countless others who spoke to the religious fervor of the region, among them William Miller, who preached that the world would come to an end in either 1843 or 1844 and drew audiences of thousands to his tent meetings in Rochester. The wonder was that considerable numbers of Millerites continued to believe, on a more flexible basis, after his second date of March 21, 1844, had passed. In the 1850s, spiritualism in a number of forms took on a vogue comparable to the excitement Millerism had aroused. In 1855, the Spiritualists were claiming a million converts throughout the world, with perhaps one-third of their number living in New York State.

One result of New York's religious fervor was that for the first time Roman Catholics outnumbered any single Protestant group. Another—more significant—was that the Burned-over District became a focus of concern about social as well as religious issues. It is no accident that the first women's rights convention was held in Seneca Falls in 1848, or that western New York was alive with concern over abolition and temperance. While the Civil War seemed to put a damper on religious extremism, the issues raised during and after that conflict were honest descendants of the earlier spiritual questions.

13

The Civil War and After

A S the North and the South drew apart on the issue of slavery, strains became evident in New York. The state was loyal to the Union cause and provided more than 500,000 men to the Union's armed forces. For the first time—excepting the Mexican War of 1846–1848—New York was not a battlefield, but the distressing riots over the draft in New York City did more damage and killed more people than the effort to keep the British off Manhattan in 1776.

Much of the South's foreign trade was financed by New York bankers; the South was a prime market for New York manufactures; and on December 15, 1860, a group of New York's business leaders signed an appeal to the South not to leave the Union. Senator William Henry Seward of New York, who had been governor from 1839 to 1843 and had narrowly missed getting the Republican nomination for the presidency in 1860, worked mightily to preserve an effective national government for Abraham Lincoln to take over on March 4, 1861, but to no avail. By February 1, seven states had withdrawn, and on February 8 the Confederate States of America was an accomplished fact.

New Yorkers' opinions ranged all across the spectrum. New York City's mayor, Fernando Wood (who was serving his third term in office even though Tammany· Hall, which had elected him in the beginning, had ousted him from its organization), had proposed that New York City secede and establish itself as a free city. Wood believed that the breakup of the United States was inevitable and that New York ought not to jeopardize its profitable trade relations with the South by taking an anti-Southern stand. Horace Greeley responded with a classic put-down: "Fernando Wood evidently wants to be a traitor; it is lack of courage only that makes him content with being a blackguard."

The Southern attack on Fort Sumter in April 1861 clarified many New Yorkers' thoughts: the Union was too precious to be allowed to disintegrate. The New York City Council voted $1,000,000 to meet recruiting expenses, and private citizens raised $2,500,000 to help the Union buy arms. Men volunteered to join the army; women volunteered to work for the U.S. Sanitary Commission, forerunner of the Red Cross, organized to assist in the care of sick and wounded soldiers and their dependent families. The militia regiments prepared to march, and the Seventh Regiment was on its way to Washington within a week. Not long afterward the Sixty-ninth Regiment, largely composed of the city's Irish, followed suit. On July 21, the first major battle of the war was fought at Bull Run, and the Union forces fell back, defeated, to the national capital. New York had a bitter taste of what the war would mean: Union casualties approached 3,000 men, and one-third of them were New Yorkers.

After the initial burst of enthusiasm, recruiting lagged. The state and counties tried to encourage enlistments by offering bonuses, and in July 1862 New York passed an inadequate draft law. But the Union needed many more men than it was getting, and in March 1863 Congress passed a draft act—the first federal draft in the nation's history. It included the odious provision that a man could get out of serving by paying $300 or by providing a substitute to take his place. Governor Horatio Seymour, a Democrat who had been highly critical of the Republican administration, complained that New York's quotas were too high, that conscription was unconstitutional, and that he expected it would lead to mob action. Some New Yorkers had been making money on war orders, but the poor had suffered from price inflation. Several strikes had been broken by em-

ployers who hired black substitutes for white workingmen. The
$300 exemption was a sham to those who did not have the
money to buy it.

In New York City the first draft lottery began at 677 Third
Avenue, on the corner of Forty-sixth Street, on Saturday, July
11. On the following Monday it was supposed to continue, but a
great mob formed in the street, mostly men from the slums of
the lower East Side. They tore up the rails of the Third Avenue
horse-car line, routed the office's small police guard, and set
fire to the building. The mob battled a group of wounded veterans who tried to help the police restore order. The Superinten-
dent of Police, John Kennedy, was beaten almost to death. For
four days rioters swirled around the city, looting, burning,
murdering. The mob burned the homes of Abolitionists and
blacks. It broke into the Negro orphan asylum on Fifth Avenue
between Forty-third and Forty-fourth streets, empty except for
one girl who had been left behind by accident when the other
children were removed for their safety. The mob beat her to
death. It beat Colonel O'Brien of the Eleventh New York Volunteers, who was in the city on a recruiting mission, and he
died of his wounds. No one could count the number of rioters;
one estimate put the figure at 70,000. On the fourth day, some
of the militia regiments that had been sent toward Gettysburg,
with Federal troops picked from Meade's army, entered the city
and restored order. More than a thousand people were dead. At
least eight thousand had been seriously hurt. More than one
hundred buildings had been destroyed by fire, with total property damage in excess of $1,500,000.

Because the riots were so horrible, they are too often remembered as the whole story of New York's part in the war. But a
month later the draft lottery proceeded without further incident.
New York State, with New York County at the top of the list,
contributed more soldiers to the Union army and produced more
supplies than did any other state. New Yorkers paid the most
taxes, bought the greatest number of war bonds, and gave the
most to the relief organizations.

Lincoln's assassination on April 14, 1865, just a few days
after the end of the war, stunned New York. When the train car-

rying the president's coffin stopped at New York City on its way to Springfield, Illinois, every building was draped in black. Lincoln's body lay in state at City Hall so that New Yorkers by the thousands could pay him their last respects.

One New Yorker not present at City Hall that day but confined by shame to his house on East Nineteenth Street was the reigning star of the New York theater, Edwin Booth, the older brother of the assassin, John Wilkes Booth. Edwin Booth's thrilling performance in *Hamlet* had run for a record-breaking one hundred performances. He had taken it to Boston, and there he had heard the appalling news of his brother's deed. Booth was only thirty-two years old: slight, black-haired, handsome, and with a rich, sonorous voice. He was an innovator, refusing to declaim the great speeches of the classic plays in the style of the day because he felt that they should be acted with a kind of realism. After Lincoln's death, Booth swore to himself that he would never again set foot on stage.

Booth's despair was perfectly understandable, but his resolve was impractical. He could not afford to retire. He had a small daughter and his mother, in addition to himself, to support. On January 3, 1866, with great trepidation, Booth reopened in *Hamlet* at the Winter Garden Theater on Broadway at Bond Street. On his appearance wearing Hamlet's dark suit of mourning, the audience gave Booth an ovation. The playgoers were determined to convince him that his brother's awful crime should have no effect upon Booth's career. His last performance was in *Hamlet* in Brooklyn in 1891.

New York emerged from the Civil War ready to explode into a new economic era. The family farm and the small, self-sustaining agricultural community began to disappear as the proliferation of railroads and roads, added to the network of canals, added to the rivers that had been in place since the the icecap melted, cut time and distance. New York was shrinking the way the world has been shrinking in the late twentieth century because of the jet airplane and the communications satellite.

The way to an urban–industrial New York was not entirely smooth; for that matter, the goal when achieved inspired considerable nostalgia for the family farm and the small, self-sustain-

ing community. In the first fifteen postwar years the state's population increased by more than a million people, immigrants
included, to 5,083,000. Not quite 2,000,000 of them lived in
the five boroughs that now comprise New York City. The
growth pattern for the state as well as for the city was continuing about as fast as the census-takers could count—approximately one million additional New York State residents every
ten years. The opportunities to build more railroads, more factories, more ships, and more office buildings seemed limitless,
provided one could raise the money to do so; and, to compound
the explosive force, hardly a year went by without an invention,
a discovery, or an innovation that was destined to add new
machines, new materials, and new processes to the tumult.

New Yorkers' imaginations expanded to meet, and in some
cases to create, the challenges. Cornelius Vanderbilt was an example. He was born in 1794 on Staten Island and worked as a
young man as a ferryboat captain until he became a steamboat
owner. He did so well in the Hudson River trade that his competitors paid him handsomely to stay off the river for ten years.
Vanderbilt set up lines on Long Island Sound sailing to Providence and Boston, and in 1849, when traffic to San Francisco
boomed on account of the Gold Rush, he built a new fleet of
ships to take advantage of that bonanza. The "Commodore"—
in honor of his ferryboat days—was rough, tough, proud of his
self-made millions, and unable to break into New York City's
high society. He lived in social isolation in his mansion on fashionable Washington Place, drove the finest carriage teams, and
initiated what later became a rich man's necessity—the private
ocean-going steam yacht. None of the hostesses who refrained
from inviting Vanderbilt to their costume balls had one. The
North Star had ten principal staterooms, a dining salon with polished marble walls, and Louis XV rosewood furniture uphol-
stered in figured velvet plush. Vanderbilt sailed to Europe on
his yacht for a long stay, taking with him several relatives, his
physician, his clergyman, and squads of servants; on his return
he was still a social outcast.

Before the Civil War, Vanderbilt had foreseen the decline of
shipping. He sold ships to buy railroads: first the New York and

Harlem, then its competitor, the Hudson River Railroad, then the New York Central. He fought hard to buy the Erie, but three other millionaires, Daniel Drew, Jay Gould, and James Fisk, defeated his effort. The Commodore went on to take control of the Lake Shore and Michigan Railroad, the Michigan Central, and the Canada Southern. His acquisitions, added together and called the New York Central, ran from New York City to Chicago. It was one of the first great systems of railroad transportation. The Commodore's son, William H. Vanderbilt, who had been his father's principal aide for some time, enlarged the line by buying control of the Chicago & North Western and large interests in the Cleveland, Columbus, Cincinnati & Indianapolis Railroad and the New York, Chicago & St. Louis line.

Another imaginative New Yorker was John Pierpont Morgan, whose father, Junius Spencer Morgan, was a partner in an international banking firm in London. J. P. worked for his father's bank in London, acted as its agent in New York during the Civil War, and in 1871 formed the firm of Drexel, Morgan & Company with Anthony J. Drexel as his partner. Much of the money to pay for the expansion of American business came from European investors, and Morgan's company, closely associated with bankers in London and Paris, enjoyed the special confidence of European investors.

It wasn't long before the Vanderbilt and Morgan stories intertwined: Morgan became the Vanderbilts' banker. After Commodore Vanderbilt's death, the New York Central got into a rate war with the Pennsylvania Railroad that threatened to ruin them both. William Vanderbilt asked Morgan to see if he could help. Morgan, having taken a leaf out of Commodore Vanderbilt's book, had a beautiful rakish black yacht, the *Corsair*. He invited the top officials of the Pennsylvania for a cruise up the Hudson. Nine hours after the yacht had left New York City she was back at her dock, and a workable peace plan had been arranged. The cutthroat competition had been ended, and Morgan's reputation as a financial wizard was on its way to becoming folklore.

Peacemaking—arranging mergers and combinations of competing companies—was J. P. Morgan's talent, and Congress was a generation away from seeing huge combinations as evil trusts so powerful that a new small firm might not have a chance to survive. Drexel, Morgan & Company, which later became J. P. Morgan & Company, arranged a great number of such mergers—perhaps fifty in all—starting with railroads and going on to help assemble corporations like U.S. Steel, International Harvester, and General Electric. Morgan himself, in a somewhat more charitable action, helped put together the Palisades Interstate Park.

Another major figure was Alfred Ely Beach, the publisher of *Scientific American* and an inventor, who thought that a solution to New York City's—or any city's—traffic problem lay underground. In 1870, Beach demonstrated the "Beach Pneumatic Road," a subway driven by air pressure through a block-long tunnel under Broadway between Warren and Murray streets. It worked well, but property owners (with some justification) feared that tunnel excavations might weaken the foundations of their buildings. A state commission, looking into the question, decided that part of the traffic could be lifted a level above the ground instead. (An elevated railway on Greenwich Street had operated for a time, starting in 1867, but the line had gone out of business.) Beach was disappointed but not crushed. He had quantities of other inventions in mind, and his magazine was doing well.

Construction of the "El" proceeded rapidly up Second, Third, Sixth, and Ninth avenues. By 1880, two of the elevated lines were extended all the way to Harlem, and that section of Manhattan began to bloom. The El got Manhattan dwellers to work and back with reasonable efficiency, but the trains were a blight everywhere they ran. They made an awful noise, which ricocheted off the buildings along the route; their steam engines threw sparks and coals onto the streets; they cut off light and air from the sidewalks and the shops beneath the tracks.

Twenty years later, in 1900, New York City started all over again on Beach's subway suggestion although it did not use his pneumatic tube design. It took fifty years, until well after the Second World War, to get rid of Manhattan's major elevated railways (the island's topography forces some lines briefly above the surface) and their scars are still visible in a good many neighborhoods. The Bronx, Brooklyn, and Queens have to struggle along with some elevated lines, component parts of the mammoth Metropolitan Transit Authority.

The winter of 1866–1867 inspired another addition to New York's transportation network. It was cold enough to freeze the rivers. New Yorkers could walk across solid ice from Manhattan to Brooklyn, but ferryboats were immobilized. The freeze reminded the city fathers that they needed a bridge to Brooklyn in fair weather as well as foul, and the New York Bridge Company, formed in April 1867, claimed that it had just the man for the difficult job of building one: John A. Roebling. He was born in Germany and came to the United States in 1831. He had built a suspension bridge over the Monongahela River at Pittsburgh and the pioneer railroad bridge over the Niagara River not far below the Falls.

Roebling explained that a suspension bridge across the East River, hanging from cables supported by great towers on the shores instead of resting on piers spaced across the river, would have the great advantage of not interfering with navigation, and his plans won the approval of Congress and the War Department in June 1869. One day in July Roebling was on a cluster of piles at the end of a ferry slip, trying to decide the precise location of the tower on the Brooklyn side, when a ferryboat docked. The impact caught his foot and crushed his boot and his toes. He developed tetanus, and a month later he was dead. His son, Washington A. Roebling, a graduate of Rensselaer Polytechnic Institute and an officer of engineers in the Union army, carried on the work.

When the free public bridge, which had cost $15,000,000, was officially opened on May 24, 1883, Mayor Seth Low of Brooklyn remarked: "The beautiful and stately structure fulfills the fondest hope. . . . The impression upon the visitor is one of astonishment that grows with every visit. No one who has been upon it can ever forget it. . . . Not one shall see it and not feel prouder to be a man.''[1] For half a century thereafter, the Brooklyn Bridge reigned supreme as the most magnificent, if

1. Quoted in David McCullough, *The Great Bridge* (New York: Simon & Schuster, 1972), p. 536.

not technically the largest, suspension bridge on earth. And it did everything its promoters had promised. It stimulated growth, provided a safe, reliable alternative to the ferries no matter how far the thermometer fell, and raised property values.

Three years after the bridge's opening, the Statue of Liberty, properly "Liberty Enlightening the World," was unveiled. It was the gift of the French to the American people, belatedly commemorating a century of American independence. Frederic Auguste Bartholdi, the Alsatian sculptor who conceived the one-hundred-fifty-two-foot lady, built the statue in Paris during the 1870s and early 1880s. The colossal copper figure was taken apart and shipped to New York in sections in 1885. As soon as it was in place, it became the symbol of welcome to every shipload of immigrants entering the harbor: one of the first things to be seen of the New World as they came up the bay, a minute or two before the bridge and the lower Manhattan skyline were quite clear. It was the landmark that every new arrival looked for.

14

Power and Influence

*O*N January 1, 1898, New York became Greater New York. Under a new charter from the state legislature, the city attained its present physical size, 320 square miles. Five counties—New York (Manhattan), the Bronx, Queens, Kings (Brooklyn), and Richmond (Staten Island)—became the five boroughs of the City of New York, united under one mayor with single departments—police, fire, education, and so on—serving the whole city.

To a large extent, unification was the result of the work of one man, a lawyer named Andrew Haswell Green. He had come to New York from Massachusetts as a fifteen-year-old boy in 1835 and had worked as a messenger for his board and keep and the munificent sum of $50 a year. He studied law, was admitted to the bar in 1844, went into practice, and became the law partner of Samuel J. Tilden, six years his senior. Green was drawn to public service: president of the Board of Education (1856); planner and commissioner of Central Park; city comptroller (1871–1876). It was Green, as comptroller, who discovered that the Tweed Ring had bankrupted the city. He borrowed from friends and associates in the emergency to pay city employees' salaries. When Tammany returned to power, Green left the city government and devoted himself to working for the Metropolitan Museum of Art, the American Museum of Natural History, the New York Zoological Society, the New York Botanical Society, and above all the Greater New York scheme—widely known by its foes and friends as "Green's Hobby."

The most powerful opposition to consolidation came from Brooklyn, which had received its city charter in 1834. Brooklyn had a character distinctly its own, and patriotic Brooklynites saw little hope of improvement in closer association with the other communities. On Brooklyn Heights stood the handsome mansions of Brooklyn's great merchants. Brooklyn had beautiful Prospect Park, splendid avenues, a new museum, a bustling downtown business section, and its own political machine—almost as crooked as Tammany and not the least bit anxious to complicate the division of its spoils. Queens and Staten Island were still collections of villages. The South Bronx and Manhattan had already joined, and the North Bronx, with no great sense of separate identity, did not fear that it would lose anything by uniting with its neighbors to the south. The Bronx also had a reason for being grateful to Green: as Central Park commissioner he had felt that overcrowding of the space might spoil the concept, and so he had been influential in putting New York's botanical garden and main zoo into the spaciousness of Bronx Park.

In 1894 the question of consolidation was put to a popular vote and passed, but so narrowly that the state legislature defeated the consolidation bill that was presented on the basis of the popular vote. In 1896, with Tammany boss Richard Croker working with upstate Republicans led by Boss Thomas C. Platt, the bill was passed, but before consolidation could become a fact a charter had to be written. When that onerous task was done in 1897 and the document was presented to the mayors for their signatures, the totally unexpected occurred: the mayor of Brooklyn approved but the mayor of New York would have none of it.

In spite of New York's veto, the state legislature passed the charter, the governor signed it, and Greater New York, with a population of 3,100,000, became a reality. The first mayor of Greater New York was Robert A. Van Wyck, a Tammany choice; in 1901 Brooklyn's Seth Low, then president of Columbia University, was elected mayor on a fusion ticket in a wave of reform. The city charter presented a host of problems from the outset—the very point that New York had endeavored to make. It was revised completely under Low, and the revised version served (if imperfectly) for the next thirty-seven years.

The physical appearance of New York City was changing rapidly, as fast as or faster than its political structure. The apartment house (not to be confused with the tenement) had grown in popularity. The very first, on Eighteenth Street between Irving Place and Third Avenue, was built right after the Civil War by Rutherford Stuyvesant, and it quickly rented to prosperous, middle-class New Yorkers despite the attitude on the part of society's Old Guard that an apartment was hardly better than a slum. (The correct dwelling for those who could afford it, but did not aspire to a mansion, was a four- or five-story brown stone; a hundred years later, numbers of New Yorkers feel just the same.) Nevertheless, apartment houses proliferated because they made it possible to stack up a large number of families in some comfort on lots that would otherwise contain only a brownstone or two. The outstanding New York City survivor of the trend is the apartment house on the north side of Seventy-second Street and Central Park West, nicknamed "the Dakota" because in 1881, when it was built, it seemed so far uptown and beyond the built-up neighborhoods that it might as well have been in Dakota Territory.

Six years later, in 1887, the architect Bradford Lee Gilbert started to build New York's first "skyscraper": the Tower Building at 50 Broadway, south of Exchange Place. It was thirteen stories tall, and called a "skyscraper" because that was the topmost sail on a clipper ship's rig. Gilbert thought of it as "a bridge truss stood on end"—an internal frame, made of steel girders, would support the unprecedented weight of the building's masonry. To demonstrate his confidence that the building could stay upright in a strong wind, Gilbert promised to use the top two floors himself.

The remodeling of New York City was more than matched by the transformations cities and town throughout the rest of the state were undergoing. Former stockades and trading posts like Oswego, Buffalo, and Rome had turned into bustling cities pushing against their limits. Their towering factory smokestacks poured pollution into the air. In every county, the county seat boasted—in addition to the courthouse—a busy business street. If it lacked one of the new-fangled department stores, like A. T. Stewart's at Ninth Street and Broadway in New York City, it had an enterprising retail merchant who meant to provide it.

At Ilion, Philo Remington, the eldest of Eliphalet Remington's three sons, was worried that the huge factory of E. Remington & Sons, which had manufactured pistols and rifles for the Union army, had excess capacity. It was making agricultural machinery and sewing machines, but one whole wing of the plant was underemployed. In 1874, Remington began to produce the first practical typewriter, designed by Christopher Latham Sholes with help from a number of men, including two of Remington's master mechanics. Mark Twain bought one almost immediately, and he loved it so much he wrote a free reverse-English testimonial for the "curiosity-breeding little joker."

The world did not accept the typewriter as quickly as Twain had. Learning to type was not the easiest process in the world, partly because Sholes and his associates had messed up the arrangement of the letters on the keyboard, not realizing that they were setting a standard for the next century and perhaps forever. Trained typists were scarce because the job paid $10 a week on the average and not many young men were interested. (Telegraph operators were men; shorthand stenographers were men; it seemed logical that typists would be men.) In 1881, the Central Branch of the Young Women's Christian Association in New York City initiated a typing class for eight young ladies. The eight graduates were immediately hired, the YWCA got hundreds of requests for more, and typewriting schools spread all over the country. It was not long before E. Remington & Sons had to increase the plant space allocated to Sholes's gadget.

All kinds of new institutions and structures were growing throughout the state. At Poughkeepsie, in 1867, Vassar Female College dropped the word "Female" from its name and became simply Vassar College—a convenience a century later when it began to admit males. Vassar, six years old at the time, was the first great college for females in the United States. At Ithaca, in 1868, Cornell opened its doors thanks to the generosity of Ezra Cornell, one of the founders of the Western Union Telegraph Company.

That same year a Brooklyn firm, the Flint Glass Company, moved to Corning because there was a considerable amount of low-cost coal in the vicinity, plus glass-sand rock; thus the foundations of the Corning Glass Company were laid. At Albany, in 1867, construction of a new capitol building got under way on the understanding that it would not cost more than $4,000,000. In 1877, two years before the first portion of the extraordinary edifice was complete, Governor Lucius Robinson remarked that the unfinished capitol was "a public calamity— without parallel for extravagance and folly."

At Rochester the Eastman Dry Plate and Film Company, which had been organized by a local young man, George Eastman, looked promising. Eastman had been convinced for some time that photography had commercial possibilities. He had invented a machine for coating dry plates, and by 1884 he was experimenting with transparent, flexible, paper-backed film. Eastman's business improved markedly after 1888 when the company introduced a simple, inexpensive camera using the paper-backed film. Eastman called it the "Kodak" and advertised it with the slogan "You push the button; we do the rest."

Troy had been a real city for quite a time—the eastern end of the Erie Canal and the site of a great arsenal making arms, ammunition, and armor plate. During the Civil War, Henry Burden's Iron Works, powered by twin blast furnaces, had been capable of producing horseshoes at the rate of 3,600 an hour. After the war, Troy grew as factory-made men's shirts, collars, and cuffs and laundry machinery set sales records. One of Troy's biggest new plants belonged to Cluett, Peabody & Company, makers of Arrow collars and cuffs and Cluett and Monarch shirts.

Buffalo, with thirty-seven miles of waterfront, was in the process of becoming a great port—which mixed good with bad, as New York City could attest—with grain distribution its specialty. It remains the state's major Great Lakes port.

Urbanization provided all kinds of excitement, but the agricultural character of New York changed slowly. The number of farms increased for a time (there were 241,000 in 1880 compared to 197,000 in 1860) and then their size grew as their numbers dwindled. The change came as New York farmers thought more and more about producing for the market, and transportation moved the market farther and farther away—or closer and closer, depending on which figure of speech you prefer. Dairy farming—butter, cheese, and milk—took the place of wheat as the state's most valuable agricultural product; as wheat lost its status, corn, oats, barley, rye, potatoes, flax, hops, and apples took on added importance. (In the Finger Lakes district and Chautauqua County, grape and wine industries developed.) Output per farm rose, and so did the efficiency of farm workers as one ingenious piece of farm machinery after another—new plows, harrows, cultivators, reapers, threshers—came off the inventors' drawing boards.

That was just as well, because the lure of the West was powerful; New York farmboys by the tens of thousand disappeared in the direction of Illinois, Michigan, Wisconsin, and beyond. (Many of their places were taken by the new waves of immigrants, some of them farmers from Italy and Poland, who thought that Buffalo *was* west.) New York's upstate population grew steadily, but most of the growth was in urban areas. People collected, like iron filings drawn to a magnet, on a line along the Erie Canal–New York Central routes—Albany, Utica, Syracuse, Rochester, and Buffalo—that was not much more than twenty-five miles wide.

Downstate, meanwhile, New York City and its environs continued to make room of some kind for immigrants: Russian Jews, Greeks, Rumanians, Poles in the 1870s and 1880s; Italians from Sicily and the area around Naples in the 1880s and 1890s. By 1890, 42 percent of New York City's population was foreign-born.

The man who opened well-to-do New York's eyes to what

was going on in its slums was an immigrant from Denmark, Jacob Riis. He had arrived at New York in 1870. After some tough experiences of his own, he became a police reporter assigned to police headquarters on Mulberry Street in the heart of Little Italy. He began to write articles about crimes against the poor instead of by them: fifteen people sleeping in two tiny bedrooms; a Mulberry Street tenement where one-third of all the babies born soon died. Riis's first book, *How The Other Half Lives*, was published in 1890. It shocked a great many well-meaning, well-to-do New Yorkers who had not realized how bad the slums were. In 1901, the city managed to pass a tenement-house law that outlawed much of what had been legal since 1879, when the "Old Law" was enacted, and the New Law served as a model for reform legislation in other cities throughout the country. The catch was that it only applied to *new* buildings in slum neighborhoods. Eight years after its passage, at least 600,000 New York City families were still living in Old Law tenements.

By 1890, the United States was well on the way to becoming the world's industrial leader and New York State was contributing about one-sixth of the nation's manufactures. In dollar value, New York's six most important manufactured products were men's clothing, women's clothing, milled flour, foundry and machine shop products, textiles, and printed and published materials.

The garment industry, holding the top two places on the list, was the offspring of the sewing machine invented in Boston in 1846 by Elias Howe and improved and popularized in New York during the 1860s by a Pittstown native, Isaac M. Singer. On the eve of the Civil War, eight times out of ten, a man's suit was made to order by a tailor. By 1880, the odds were reduced to five times out of ten; twenty years later, after the introduction of half sizes and odd sizes, a tailor-made suit was unnecessary. Sewing machines called for the invention of a host of related tools, and inventors obliged. Tailors had cut a single layer of fabric according to a pattern. Cutting machines could slice through forty layers of woolen cloth at one clip, producing, say, forty backs for forty size 36 Regular jackets in the twinkling of an eye. At the turn of the century New York State was producing 45 percent of the men's clothing for the nation, and skilled cutters were highly regarded because a clumsy error, multiplied by forty, could cost a garment manufacturer his Cluett shirt.

The great trouble with the garment industry was the nightmarish conditions under which many of its employees worked. Men, women, and as often as not children worked painfully long hours, either at home or in "sweatshops," as the industry's crowded, rickety, airless factory and loft buildings were called. Women regularly worked six days a week, and night shifts in addition. Children as young as seven or eight were employed. A manufacturer could divide the making of any given garment into thirty or forty operations, most of them simple enough to require minimal training; contractors, acting as agents, would bid on each part of the whole job; and the less the contractor paid workers per piece, the better off he would be. Immigrants in the slums were grateful to contractors for the opportunity to earn a pittance.

Trade unions made some progress in New York. Samuel Gompers, the son of a Dutch Jew, who had arrived with his family from London in 1863, had worked as a cigarmaker all day long while getting an education by attending Cooper Union's free night classes. He also listened carefully, while he rolled cigars, to the books and periodicals that were read aloud in cigarmakers' shops. The workers bought them with a common fund and took turns reading. Gompers became the president of the cigarmakers' union Local 144 and in 1886 president of the newly formed American Federation of Labor. Nine years earlier, in 1877, the cigarmakers' union had engaged in a long, bitter, and unsuccessful strike against the tenement-house sweatlabor system, and for decades the unions had been frightening employers and the public alike by preaching varieties of (mostly German) socialist doctrine. Gompers preached strict adherence to union objectives: higher wages, shorter hours, better working conditions.

In 1900, the AF of L chartered the International Ladies Garment Workers' Union. Yet in spite of the efforts of union leaders, social workers, reformers, and editorial writers, garment-industry employees were cruelly exploited. It took a dismal tragedy to bring a measure of reform. On Saturday, March 25, 1911, the Triangle Waist Company, occupying the top three floors of a ten-story building on Washington Place, was working at full capacity. Six hundred women, most between thirteen and twenty-three years old, were trapped by a fire that swept through the eighth, ninth, and tenth floors. There were no sprinklers, and the door to the stairs was locked. When fire engines arrived, their ladders reached only to the sixth floor. One hundred forty-one persons, including sixteen men employees, died, some because they jumped to escape the flames. New York grieved: a procession of more than 100,000 followed hearses to Mount Zion Cemetery in Queens. Protest meetings were held. A state investigating commission was appointed, with Senator Robert F. Wagner as chairman and Assemblyman Alfred E. Smith as vice chairman. Eventually the building and factory laws, especially their fire-safety regulations, were greatly improved.

New York influenced what Americans wore simply by making their clothes for them. Other New York influences were transmitted in more subtle ways. New York was in a position to give lessons in political corruption to a good many other states.

By the end of the Civil War, William Marcy Tweed, son of a Scottish-born furniture maker, was the Grand Sachem of Tammany and in almost total control of New York City politics. His friends as well as his enemies called him "Boss" Tweed without offending him, and he worked with a group of cronies that included John T. Hoffman, the ex-mayor; Oakey Hall, the mayor, known as "Elegant Oakey" on account of his fashionable clothes; Richard B. ("Slippery Dick") Connolly, the comptroller; Peter B. ("Brains") Sweeney, the chamberlain; and several corrupt judges. Tweed's *modus operandi* was to accept bribes. On a small scale, as a member of the Board of Education, Tweed ripped off public school teachers; the bribe price for a job was $75. In all fairness, it should be said that Tweed paid bribes, too. He bought his own election to the State Senate in 1867 and Hoffman's election to the governorship in 1868. He

bought a new charter for New York City in 1870 (his man hand-
ing out bribes in Albany to assemblymen was said to have a
$600,000 budget for the purpose) that made it ridiculously easy
for Tweed to loot the City's treasury in the name of "reform."

Tweed was widely acclaimed as a benefactor of the poor,
which was true enough on the eve of elections, and there was
some thought of erecting a statue of him in New York Harbor.
Tweed's monument became instead the Criminal Court Building
at the north end of City Hall Park, which cost the city
$12,500,000 instead of the $850,000 that had been anticipated.
Much of the difference went into the Tweed Ring's pockets.
The total amount that Tweed and his colleagues stole from
New York City was probably no more than $200,000,000, be-
cause Tweed was arrested and indicted before the end of 1872.

The editor of the *New York Times,* an up-and-coming newspaper, founded in 1851, had announced in its first issue that
"we do not mean to write as if we were in a passion—unless
that shall really be the case; and we shall make it a point to get
into a passion as rarely as possible." It got into a passion about
Tweed. Thomas Nast, a staff contributor to *Harper's Weekly,*
began in 1869 to draw devastating anti-Tweed cartoons. And
the thieves had a falling out: a Tammany sheriff, Jimmy
O'Brien, aggrieved because he thought Tweed had done him out
of a lot of money, went to the *Times* with documentary proof of
corruption in the state comptroller's office. The newspaper
printed the material. Samuel J. Tilden, the state Democratic
party chairman, who had not wanted to break with Tweed until
the evidence against him was incontrovertible, finally entered
the battle and in short order became the leader of the anti-Tweed
forces. Considering the multitude of persons who had gone
along with Tweed, the number punished was small—none of the
Republican assemblymen who had taken his bribes, for instance, was sent to jail. Mayor Hall was saved by a hung jury.
Sweeney and Connolly escaped to Europe. Tweed was sentenced to twelve years; got out on a technicality; was arrested a
second time; escaped the jail and fled the country; was arrested
a third time; and died in the Ludlow Street jail in 1878.

15

Cultural Forces at Work

IN 1874, on the shores of beautiful Lake Chautauqua in Chautauqua County, some key features of popular adult education had their beginnings. A Methodist clergyman, the Reverend John A. Vincent, had the idea of adding a few lectures in science and the humanities to the practical short summer training program for Sunday School teachers he had organized. Vincent was helped and encouraged by an Akron, Ohio, inventor and farm-implement manufacturer, Lewis Miller, an enthusiast for the idea that education and recreation combined extremely well. Vincent and Miller called their program, which lasted two weeks in August, the Chautauqua Assembly, and the first students stayed in a simple sort of camp. The Chautauqua idea, which was developed with uncommon speed, caught fire and blazed into a remarkable complex of activity. The little camp grew into a permanent summer colony; the course was lengthened first to three weeks and then to two months, as new subjects were added. In its fifth year, under the guiding hand of William Rainey Harper (who became the first president of the University of Chicago in 1892), a home-study reading program or correspondence course called The Literary and Scientific Circle was offered. It immediately attracted 7,000 subscribers. (In later years, when the Chautauqua movement was at its zenith, as many as 25,000 readers were enrolled in the course.)

The Assembly grew year after year, adding a school for

149

teachers of secular subjects; schools of languages, of mathematics and sciences, of music, arts, crafts, and physical education; and, as Assembly attendance grew, lecture halls, a theater, a library, gymnasiums, club houses, and a memorial church. By the time of the Great Depression, when the Chautauqua Assemblies lost many of their visitors, the idea of education combined with recreation and "pure, wholesome entertainment" was drawing 45,000 student-vacationers each season.

After 1900, the Chautauqua phenomenon was so well known, and the Assembly so well attended, that it could attract and pay for the nation's best-known lecturers. And since not everyone could visit Lake Chautauqua from late June to late August, a perceptive agent put Chautauqua on the road. A digest-sized sample of the real thing, two or three sessions a day held in a circus-style tent featuring improving lectures, music, and drama, travelled from town to town. A magazine, the *Chautauquan,* was published. The Chautauqua Book-A-Month Club for a time distributed good books of a wholesome sort to as many as 500,000 members. The club may have been in the long run Chautauqua's most influential facet, for it is hard to imagine that Harry Scherman, when he originated the Book-of-the-Month Club in 1926, did not appreciate the triumph the Book-A-Month Club had achieved.

In the two decades after the turn of the century, hundreds of local assemblies, modeled to some degree after the Chautauqua original, appeared throughout the United States and Canada. Many of them called themselves "chautauquas," as if it were a generic term, and there is no doubt that their popularity was a help to those men and women who were arguing the case for public adult education on a year-round basis. The wave of new immigrants pouring into New York added urgency to the idea, and by 1912 some 200,000 adults, many of them foreign-born, were studying in continuation, factory, and evening schools in the state—a program that, with some ups and downs, has been expanding ever since. Chautauqua itself, now called The Chautauqua Institution, is still very much alive and attracts thousands of visitors every summer to its concerts, plays, operas, ballets, summer-school courses, and daily lectures.

While Chautauqua pioneers were revealing the power of enlightenment and entertainment in a judicious mixture, New York newspapers were showing the nation some interesting possibilities in styles of daily journalism—but at almost the opposite end of the ethical scale. In 1883, a skinny thirty-six-year-old from St. Louis bought the *New York World* from Jay Gould. His name was Joseph Pulitzer, and he had earned his passage to the United States by enlisting in the Union army at Hamburg, Germany. In St. Louis he worked as a reporter on the *Westliche Post,* a German-language daily; then he bought the bankrupt *St. Louis Staats-Zeitung* for peanuts and in next to no time had sold its Associated Press franchise to the *St. Louis Daily Globe* for enough more than peanuts to pay his own way through law school. Two years as a lawyer reminded him that journalism was an intriguing occupation. Pulitzer bought the *Dispatch* and the *Post,* merged them, and as publisher of the *Post-Dispatch* made a great success in five years as a crusader against local political corruption.

On acquiring the *World,* Pulitzer explained that the paper would oppose the "aristocracy of money"; its mission was to become the organ of the *true* American aristocrat, the working man. And indeed the *World's* editorial page urged heavy taxation of luxuries, inheritances, large incomes, and privileged corporations, along with stiff punishments for corrupt politicians and purchasers of votes. The other pages were crammed with crime, sex, bold headlines, stunning exposés, photographs, cartoons, and—as soon as Pulitzer had invented the form—comic strips in color. (In 1895, while experimenting with a new color press, Pulitzer added a spot of yellow ink to the nightshirt of a cartoon's prototypical bad-boy character, an Irish slum urchin, and the strip soon became famous as "The Yellow Kid." In time, the *World's* recipe for vulgar sensationalism came to be called "yellow journalism," a term of opprobrium.) Pulitzer also hired New York's best reporters. The *World's* international news, if a reader could find it, was unsurpassed for excellence. All the New York aristocrats—monied, true, and in-between— were soon reading the *World,* including many who preferred the editorial outlook of the conservative *Evening Post.* By 1892, the combined circulation of the *World* and the *Evening World* was 374,000, larger than any two competitors and more profitable as well.

Pulitzer had barely completed his conquest of New York City newspaper publishing when, in 1895, a tall, pallid, thirty-two-year-old Californian named William Randolph Hearst showed up in New York. He believed that he could beat the *World* at its own game. Hearst's father, who had crossed the plains on foot to California in 1850, had made millions in mine speculations and purchased the *San Francisco Examiner* for his son. William Randolph, by emulating and even enlarging upon Pulitzer's innovations, had made the *Examiner* very popular. Hearst bought the *New York Journal*, brought some of his staff from San Francisco, and hired a number of the *World's* best people away—including Richard Outcault, creator of "The Yellow Kid." (The *World* survived that stab in the back by having another artist, George B. Luks, draw the strip.)

Hearst managed to make the *Journal* a shade or two yellower than the *World*, although in the competition the *World* got yellower than ever before. The *Journal's* first big story concerned the marriage of Consuelo Vanderbilt, the Commodore's great-granddaughter, to the Duke of Marlborough; the weddings, parties, feuds, and scandals of high society built circulation. Much later, when Hearst had acquired a great chain of newspapers and magazines, their editorial policy was conservative; but in the 1890s the *Journal* defended labor unions, denounced the trusts, and argued that municipal ownership of the gas and electric companies was the only way New Yorkers could hope to avoid paying outrageously high rates.

Pulitzer, ill and going blind, had retired from direct management of the *World*, and when the *Journal* began to print lurid stories about the war in Cuba—a revolution against Spain that had started in 1895—the *World* did its best to beat the *Journal*. Both papers printed fictitious Spanish atrocity stories, coupled with pleas for United States aid to the brave Cubans and help for the American owners of Cuban plantations and sugar mills whose property was being destroyed by the civil war. It was difficult for New Yorkers to believe that *both* papers were printing lies. Americans all over the country were horrified by the cruelties the Spanish generals were supposed to be practicing. President William McKinley, who had been following his predecessor Grover Cleveland's policy of neutrality, sent the battleship *Maine* to Havana to "protect American interests," which were perhaps $50,000,000 of invested capital and annual trade worth about twice that much. On February 15, 1898, the *Maine* blew up in the harbor at Havana, killing two officers and 258 members of the crew. No one knew what caused the explosion, but the headline-sized slogan "Remember The *Maine*" swept across the country. By April 19, 1898, the United States and Spain were at war. Hostilities were over in four months, but total American casualties, dead and wounded, came to 4,108.

Pulitzer then reversed the direction the *World* had taken. It abandoned sensationalism, along with the idea of representing the working classes, and it turned into an extremely literate, well-informed newspaper with a fine editorial page—a favorite of New Yorkers, who supported liberal and democratic ideas whether they worked or not. The real victor in the *Journal*'s assault upon the *World* was the *New York Times,* which had been failing until Adolph S. Ochs, the publisher of the *Chattanooga* (Tennessee) *Times,* took over its management in 1896. The *Times* reported the war, and everything else, in a sober, responsible manner, true to its two slogans, "All the news that's fit to print," and "It does not soil the breakfast cloth." In addition to being clean, Ochs insisted that the *Times*'s editorial opinions should be subordinate to accurate news, even if the news ran directly against his editorial writers' preferences. He rejected advertising that seemed to him misleading or improper. His fussiness over the integrity of the *Times,* it later appeared, was good journalism.

The last third of the nineteenth century also saw a remarkable proliferation of magazines, monthly and weekly: from 600 in 1850 to 3,000 in 1890. Most of them were business and professional periodicals. Many of the best of the several that aspired to a general audience followed, more or less, in the footsteps of *Harper's New Monthly Magazine,* which the book publishing firm of Harper & Brothers had started in 1850. It was a handsome 144-page publication, lavishly illustrated with woodcuts, carrying serial presentations of British and American novels. *Scribner's Magazine,* founded in 1870, was another in the same class, along with *Galaxy, Frank Leslie's Popular Monthly, The Nation* (founded by Edwin Lawrence Godkin), *The Century, Putnam's,* and James Russell Lowell's *Atlantic Monthly.* All but the last, which had no illustrations and may have been the most distinguished of the lot, were published in New York. They carried almost no advertising, apart from book announcements, because advertising was considered degrading. (The advertising business, which was destined to become more profitable than the magazine business, was waiting for a trade magazine—*Printer's Ink*—in 1911 to champion the radical notion of truth in advertising.)

McClure's Magazine, founded in 1893, turned magazine publishing into new directions. It was stuffed with advertising. Cheap photoengraving had replaced expensive woodcuts so that, in addition to running a wealth of illustrations, *McClure's* was able to charge ten cents a copy rather than the thirty-five cents Americans had come to expect to pay. Best of all, McClure's writers, including Lincoln Steffens, Ida Tarbell, and Ray Stannard Baker, invented "muckraking." This early form of investigative reporting perfectly matched in style and content the mood of hundreds of thousands of literate Americans who were disgusted with railroad financiers' shenanigans (Baker), municipal corruption and the alliances between politics and big business (Steffens), and ruthless corporate ethics (Tarbell). *McClure's* was the country's first mass-circulation magazine (350,000), and it inspired a number of other general magazines to expose wrongs that in many cases were not yet specifically against the law. Among those inspired were *Collier's,* which published Mark Sullivan's attack on patent medicine frauds and Upton Sinclair's account of frightful conditions in the meat-packing industry; *Cosmopolitan; Everybody's;* the *American Magazine;* and *Munsey's,* which by 1900 had achieved a circulation of 650,000. It was more than pure coincidence that Congress passed the Pure Food and Drug Act and the Meat Inspection Act in 1906 and that the Seventeenth Amendment, providing for the direct election of United States senators, was ratified in 1913.

The pleasures and palaces of the very rich in New York City—the delight of yellow journalism and an inspiration to the muckrakers—had a considerable impact throughout the United States: they were imitated in cities like Pittsburgh, Chicago, and San Francisco. As the fantastic chateaux and palaces of the Astors, Stewarts, Vanderbilts, Goulds, Carnegies, Fricks, Harknesses, and Guggenheims stretched north from Twenty-third Street along Fifth Avenue, it was hard to remember that there were very few millionaires who could afford a Fifth Avenue mansion and probably no more than four thousand millionaires in the whole country. With a handful of exceptions, the mansions have all been torn down.

What has proved more durable than Victorian Gothic and French Renaissance Eclectic houses are the institutions for public pleasures that were founded for the most part by post-Civil War fortunes. For 150 years, New York had not had a first-class museum of fine arts. Not long after the Civil War, John Jay, a son of the Supreme Court justice, proposed to his fellow Union League Club members that they lead the way toward a permanent gallery of art, and they concurred. The Art Committee of the Club, headed by publisher George Palmer Putnam, included a number of artists as well as an art dealer, Samuel P. Avery, who was helping several millionaires acquire private collections of their own. As a result, the Metropolitan Museum of Art was organized in 1870, with John Taylor Johnston as president and an all-star board of trustees that included painters John F. Kensett and Eastman Johnson, sculptor J. Q. A. Ward, architect Richard Morris Hunt, and Frederick Law Olmsted.

Since Johnston was a collector who had opened his private gallery over the stable of his mansion on Fifth Avenue and Eighth Street to the public one day a week and was greatly interested in living American artists—his collection included Frederick E. Church's "Niagara" and Winslow Homer's "Prisoners from the Front"—quite a few living American artists hoped that the Metropolitan might concentrate on contemporary American art. They were disappointed. Long before there was a museum or a collection, the Metropolitan was devoted to forming a more or less complete collection of objects representing the history of art, and Johnston went to work buying. France and Germany were at war, and two large European private collections—174 paintings, mostly Dutch and Flemish—had come on the market. Johnston agreed with a member of his executive committee, William T. Blodgett, that the Metropolitan needed the canvases, although they cost considerably more than the total that had been contributed for acquisitions. In time, the trustees agreed that Blodgett and Johnston had done reasonably well.

In 1872, the museum opened in a rented brownstone on Fifth Avenue near Fifty-third Street, and, as Johnston wrote, "People were generally surprised, and agreeably so, to find what we had."[1] In 1880 the Metropolitan's own building, a small fragment of the present-day leviathan, designed by Calvert Vaux, was ready for occupancy. Meanwhile, for $60,000, Johnston had bought a fantastic collection of 10,000 antiquities that had been excavated on the island of Cyprus by the American consul there, General Louis Palma di Cesnola. The general was an Italian army officer who had come to the United States and had served in the Union army. Although he was not an archeologist by training, he had spent his six years on Cyprus digging with professional ardor. According to one estimate, he had opened up eight thousand Phoenician, Greek, Assyrian, and Egyptian tombs in addition to a Temple of Venus.

No sooner had the museum opened in its new quarters, with Cesnola as its director, than it was hit by scandal. A French antiques dealer charged that the Cesnola collection was full of fakes: that false restorations and repairs had been made and that the patina on the bronzes was artificial. Two of the statues, an art critic wrote, were "a fradulent patchwork of unrelated parts." Richard Watson Gilder, in a twelve-page editorial in *The Century,* tore Cesnola to pieces. Cesnola continued as director until his death in 1904, and the nationwide controversy

1. Quoted in Lloyd Morris, *Incredible New York* (New York: Random House, 1951), p. 158.

did wonders for the Museum's attendance figures. The entire United States was made aware, at least tangentially, that a proper art museum was something an up-to-date metropolis should cherish. Upstate cities understood: The Albright Art Gallery opened in Buffalo in 1901 and the University of Rochester's Memorial Art Gallery in 1904.

About the same time, acting on an impulse that was similar to John Jay's, a young man from Maine named Albert S. Bickmore talked another group of well-to-do New Yorkers into starting the American Museum of Natural History. Its first new building, on the west side of Central Park at about Seventy-ninth Street, opened in 1877.

In 1883, the Metropolitan Opera House at Thirty-ninth Street and Broadway opened its doors and a battle was engaged, although it was not entirely evident at the gala first-night festivities. The Academy of Music on Fourteenth Street, which had opened in 1854, was the traditional home of New York City opera, and its eighteen boxes were fully subscribed by New Yorkers who were rich in 1854 (or earlier). The social value of a well-placed opera box at the Academy was incalculable. (A $30,000 offer, however, had been turned down.) The newer millionaires and their wives—the Morgans, Vanderbilts, Bakers, Rockefellers, and Whitneys—could not bear the shortage. Mrs. William K. Vanderbilt led the campaign for a new opera house. Its architect, Josiah C. Cady, sympathetic to his clients' problems, suggested three tiers of thirty-six boxes apiece. (On reflection, the topmost tier was eliminated, leaving only what envious newspapermen liked to call "The Golden Horseshoe" and "The Diamond Horseshoe.") The Metropolitan Opera defeated the Academy easily, although by the end of its first season it had run up a $600,000 deficit. After the 1884–85 season, opera at the Academy was finished.

Dr. Leopold Damrosch, who had founded the Oratorio Society and the New York Symphony Orchestra, suggested that Wagnerian opera (which he adored) could be done without great stars and with himself as conductor for much less money than the Metropolitan was spending. New York was introduced to the complete cycle of the *Ring des Nibelungen, Tristan und*

Isolde, and *Die Meistersinger.* If the boxholders minded, their displeasure was concealed. Walter Damrosch, one of Dr. Damrosch's sons, who assisted his father and was assuming some of his conducting posts, helped persuade Andrew Carnegie that New York needed a first-class symphonic hall. Carnegie was the owner of the Homestead Steel Works and in control of seven other other steel mills, and he agreed. He had written an article called "Wealth" for the *North American Review* explaining that rich men should distribute their fortunes for the "improvement of mankind." (Before he was done, Carnegie distributed at least $350,000,000.) In 1891, Carnegie Hall, at Fifty-seventh Street and Seventh Avenue, opened its doors: a true grace note to New York's cultural life.

16

A Time for Reform

$\mathcal{M}$ORE than cultural life matured in late-nineteenth-century New York. There was a change in political morality after Boss Tweed's downfall. Tammany remained as goal-directed, as powerful, and almost as brazen as before, but crude corruption had gone out of style. Cynical political jokes did not seem funny, while sober reform and dedicated reformers looked attractive rather than comic to large numbers of New York voters. For a generation—from 1875 to 1895—a number of able Democrats governed the state, including Samuel J. Tilden, Tweed's principal prosecutor; Grover Cleveland, previously the reform mayor of Buffalo; and David B. Hill, a wizard at administration who had been the mayor of Elmira. Democratic governors, much of the time, were confronted by legislatures that the Republicans dominated or controlled. In spite of divisions, a measure of progress was achieved: a dab of civil service reform, a measure of control over the great insurance companies, some amelioration of the mistreatment of New York employees by New York employers (including a prohibition against employment of children under thirteen in factories).

Then, from 1895 to 1910, the Republicans had their turns at the governorship. Their success was a demonstration of the great strength of the Republican party boss, Thomas C. Platt of Oswego. A druggist who had switched to banking, he had become president of the Tioga County National Bank and had done well as a speculator in Michigan timber land. Platt was a sophisticated political leader. He understood, among many realities, that New York's Republicans could not afford to let the Democrats do all the talking about reform, as if virtue had become a Democratic monopoly; and in 1898 Platt felt he badly needed a gubernatorial candidate who could not be associated at all with recent Republican scandals. He turned, against the advice of many of his colleagues, to Colonel Theodore Roosevelt, a war hero whose dismounted Rough Riders had taken Kettle Hill outside Santiago, Cuba, on July 1.

Roosevelt was forty years old. He had had no doubts about the propriety of the war with Spain, and with his friend Leonard Wood, President McKinley's physician, he had raised and equipped his own volunteer cavalry regiment for the expedition to Cuba. Roosevelt was an authentic national hero and much more: he had served in Albany as assemblyman from New York City's 21st District; he had campaigned, unsuccessfully, to be New York's mayor; he had served as United States Civil Service commissioner, New York City police commissioner, and assistant secretary of the navy; and he had also made time to write seven history books, including his well-regarded four-volume *Winning of The West*. His zeal, his vitality, his egotism, and his devotion to reform were all beyond question. Roosevelt was pleased to run for the governorship, and he campaigned vigorously across the state with an escort of his Rough Riders. To Platt's pleasure, Roosevelt won the election, although his winning margin was much narrower than Platt would have wished.

Roosevelt's independent attitude toward Platt's political machine was evident from the start, and he did not become any less independent after he moved into the governor's mansion. He was a competent governor who battled with the political spoils system and secured passage of a law compelling public-service corporations to pay reasonable taxes, but there was more talk in Albany about reform than there was reform legislation enacted. Governor Roosevelt's disdain for Boss Platt's advice and counsel was conspicuous. Platt found that annoying. He got rid of Roosevelt fairly easily in 1900 by maneuvering him into accepting the Republican nomination for the vice presidency as McKinley's running mate. Roosevelt was downcast—the vice presidency then amounted to even less than it does today—but still he campaigned so vigorously for the ticket that McKinley hardly needed to campaign at all.

The country was prosperous, and the McKinley–Roosevelt combination won easily. Then, on September 6, 1901, an anarchist named Leon Czolgosz shot President McKinley during a public reception at the Pan-American Exposition at Buffalo. McKinley died eight days later. Roosevelt hurried to Buffalo from the Adirondacks and was promptly sworn in. "It shall be my aim," Roosevelt said on taking the oath of office, "to continue, absolutely unbroken, the policy of President McKinley for the peace, the prosperity, and the honor of our beloved country." At the end of his first week in office, Roosevelt told a congressman: "I am going to be President of the United States and not of any section; I don't care for sections or sectional lines; if I cannot find Republicans, I am going to appoint Democrats."[1] He promptly appointed an independent Republican—almost as bad from Platt's point of view as a Democrat—collector of the Port of New York. The president was saying, in effect, that he would be his own dispenser of federal patronage in New York State, thus taking away a key element of Platt's accumulated power.

The Democrats won the governorship in 1910 with John A. Dix after Governor Charles Evans Hughes, the handsome Republican who had become celebrated as counsel for the commission that had investigated the life-insurance companies in 1905–1906, was appointed to the Supreme Court. They won again in 1912 with a Tammany veteran, William Sulzer, who then attempted to defy Tammany boss Charles E. Murphy and got himself impeached for his audacity. The Republicans promptly recaptured the governorship in 1914 by electing Charles S. Whitman, a crusading district attorney. Although the two parties seemed to be tossing the governorship back and

---

1. Quoted in Mark Sullivan, *Our Times,* Vol. 2, *America Finding Herself* (New York: Charles Scribner's Sons, 1927), pp. 393–394.

forth like a hot potato, and the incumbents were preoccupied by fighting the legislature much of the time, a series of pace-setting labor laws was passed. Most of the credit belonged to the Democratic leaders in the Senate and the Assembly—the two remarkable men who had run the Triangle Waist Company investigation, Robert F. Wagner and Alfred E. Smith.

The United States entered World War I on April 6, 1917, nearly three years after the assassination at Sarajevo of the Archduke Franz Ferdinand, the heir to the Austro-Hungarian Empire. New York's importance as a port—a distinction New Yorkers often forget between wars—was emphasized by a jam of neutral ships taking refuge from the battle between German submarines and the British navy in the Atlantic. Millions of dollars' worth of supplies were shipped through New York to Great Britain and France.

The main loading point for ammunition shipments was a mile-long pier called Black Tom that jutted into the harbor from Jersey City, behind the Statue of Liberty. Early on the morning of July 31, 1916, in a three-hour series of explosions, two million pounds of powder and artillery shells exploded and burned. The blast effect did damage for twenty-five miles—half the windows in the Custom House on Bowling Green were shattered—although, surprisingly, only seven people were killed. In effect, the war had reached New York prematurely. New Yorkers were convinced that German saboteurs had done the deed, for strong pro-Allied sentiments had replaced the earlier convictions that neutrality was the country's proper course. If that was true, it was never proved, despite investigations that went on for years after the war was over.

One month after the United States's declaration of war, ten million American men between the ages of 21 and 30 registered for the draft. New York State, led by New York City, put more men in uniform than any other state—which was only fair, since New York had more draft-age men than any other state. New York also purchased 25 percent of all the war bonds sold to finance the war effort, and New Yorkers' contributions to the Red Cross exceeded all others'.

Among the draftees from Manhattan was a small twenty-nine-year-old songwriter, Irving Berlin. He was different from most of the other privates at Camp Upton, the reception center at Yaphank, Long Island: Berlin was rich and famous. He had written "Alexander's Ragtime Band" and several other ragtime hits to which New York, with the entire country, had been dancing the one-step, the two-step, the turkey trot, the bunny-hug, the grizzly bear, and the fox trot. His sergeant did not care: like all the other draftees, Berlin had to get up at 5:45 A.M., make his bed, and stumble out of his barracks in the dark for roll call in the Company street.

Luckily for Berlin, the camp's commander, Major General Franklin Bell, was trying to raise $35,000 to build a service center, and he assigned Berlin the job of producing a show to make some money. As an encouragement, Bell promoted Berlin to sergeant. Berlin responded by writing an original revue that he called *Yip, Yip, Yaphank.* He rehearsed a cast of 227 soldiers and moved the show from Long Island to the Century Theater on Broadway. Before its run ended, it had earned $80,000. Its hit number, sung by Sgt. Berlin, was the wistful song "Oh, How I Hate To Get Up In The Morning."

For the next four decades Berlin poured forth a cascade of hit musicals: the *Music Box Revues,* the *Ziegfeld Follies, Annie Get Your Gun, Miss Liberty, Call Me Madam,* and many more. In all, he wrote the words and music for some eight hundred songs. In 1942, a quarter of a century after *Yip, Yip, Yaphank,* Berlin was a little old to reenlist, but he did want to do something. He packed his suitcase and moved to Camp Upton, once again a reception center for new soldiers. He wanted to listen, observe, and get an impression of the new generation of raw recruits. Then he composed a second musical that, like the first, caught the essence of basic training days and called it *This Is The Army.* Its proceeds went to Army Relief, and it raised not $80,000 but $10,000,000. One number stopped the show. It was Irving Berlin, dressed in his World War I uniform and still looking less than perfectly happy, singing "Oh, How I Hate To Get Up In The Morning."

Most of the soldiers who followed General John J. Pershing up Fifth Avenue in the great victory parade in September 1919 felt reasonably confident that the war to end wars had succeeded and that the world could indeed be considered safe for democracy. If they were wrong, many felt, it was time to stop worrying about Europe's fate; they had had enough of battle, enough of the idealism, the moral uplift, and the rhetoric about reform that had begun in Roosevelt's time and had been continued under President Woodrow Wilson. They were less interested in a crusade for a world order based on peace and justice under a League of Nations than in getting back to leading their own lives, so rudely interrupted. The cost of living had risen 79 percent during the war, and one of the evils of inflation—as the veterans' grandchildren learned half a century later—is its intrusiveness. Even those who are moderately well off find it difficult to think beyond their private budget struggles.

The government had encouraged unionization as a way of keeping war production at the highest possible level, and union members had been led to believe that when peace came higher wages and better working conditions were sure to follow. The soaring prices of almost everything robbed wage raises of their meaning. A wave of strikes occurred. The streetcar workers, the dress- and waistmakers, the cloak and suitmakers, the cigarmakers, and the longshoremen, printers, subway workers, and actors, among others, walked off their jobs. Labor unrest frightened a large proportion of those New Yorkers who were not themselves on strike, especially the people who thought the strikes were a tactical part of the new Communist objective, world revolution. The national membership of the Communist party, the Communist Labor party, and the Socialist party, added together, was less than 100,000 (and adding them together would have offended all three). On the other hand, the tiny minority of revolutionaries that had taken over Russia seemed to have achieved a miracle.

New York City undoubtedly housed more left-wing radicals than any other city in the United States, at least a handful of supporters for every known subversive philosophy, and some of them were foreign-born. New York's mayor, John Hylan, forbade the display of the Red flag on the city's streets. The Socialists—who were opposed to revolution—tried to meet in

Madison Square Garden and a near-riot developed. Anarchists mailed bombs in small brown paper packages at a New York City post office to Mayor Hylan, United States attorney general A. Mitchell Palmer, J. P. Morgan, Supreme Court Justice Oliver Wendell Holmes, Senator Thomas H. Hardwick of Georgia, and a number of others: seventeen in all. Sixteen of the bombs were found before they could do any damage, but the seventeenth, addressed to Senator Hardwick, was delivered and exploded, seriously hurting the maid who was opening it. Six weeks later the anarchists exploded bombs in seven cities, and one of them damaged the front of Palmer's Washington, D.C., home.

Palmer, who had a reputation as a progressive and a supporter of such liberal goals as the League of Nations, women's suffrage, and child-labor legislation, was under tremendous pressure from public opinion, Congress, and the nation's press to do something. He hesitated. After a few weeks he established a General Intelligence Division within the Department of Justice, with J. Edgar Hoover at its head, to collect information about clandestine radical activities. That satisfied hardly anyone.

Starting in November 1919, Justice Department agents began a nationwide series of raids on what were supposed to be the known meeting places of "alien radicals," with plans to deport them. Palmer's men expected to discover quantities of explosives. They found none. But they did succeed in arresting some 6,000 people, including more than 200 New Yorkers, on suspicion that they were alien Communists. Many of them were citizens, not subject to deportation. Many of them were aliens, but not radicals. A few hundred out of the thousands arrested were deported, mostly on purely technical grounds.

New Yorkers, like other Americans, seemed strangely indifferent to the outrageous civil-liberties violations the Palmer raids involved. Some prominent lawyers objected. The liberal press, including New York's *The Nation* and its five-year-old competitor *The New Republic,* protested editorially. The National Popular Government League published a sobering report on "Illegal Practices of the United States Department of Justice." But the New York State Assembly, over Governor Al

Smith's objection, refused to permit the seating of five Socialist party members elected from New York City.

Palmer, who had started to dream that he might win the 1920 Democratic presidential nomination, tried to keep his crusade bubbling by predicting a gigantic terrorist rally on May Day, 1920. The New York City police were put on twenty-four-hour duty, with federal troops on a standby alert. May Day came and May Day went without any incident, and suddenly Palmer appeared ridiculous. Four months later, a canvas-covered wagon exploded at Wall and Nassau streets, opposite the Morgan bank and not far from the New York Stock Exchange, killing 35 persons and injuring 130. No one imagined that the Communist revolution was starting; New Yorkers assumed that the bombing was a madman's work. (They were undoubtedly right, but no one knows who the driver of the lethal wagon was. He walked away, seconds before the blast, and was never caught.)

In two decades New York State's population had grown considerably, from 6,500,000 in 1900 to 10,000,000 in 1920. Most of the increase was in the cities and their adjacent suburbs—the "standard metropolitan statistical areas," as the Bureau of the Census now calls them. The New York area (including Nassau, Rockland, and Westchester counties) was the biggest, the Buffalo area (including Erie and Niagara counties) second. Then, in order, came Rochester (Monroe, Livingston, Wayne, and Orleans), Albany–Schnectady–Troy (Albany, Schnectady, Rensselaer, and Saratoga), Syracuse (Onondaga, Madison, Oswego), Utica–Rome (Oneida, Herkimer), and Binghamton (Broome and Tioga).

Before the war, the United States had been taking in about a million immigrants a year. Many of them, as always, had ventured no farther from the Statue of Liberty than New York City. After the war, with postwar Europe in turmoil, additional millions wanted to get to the United States if they could, and hundreds of thousands could: 110,000 in 1919, 430,000 in 1920, and 805,000 in 1921. Congress was frightened by this accelerating influx. The lasting effect of the Red Scare fantasies was the notion, widely held, that radicalism in the land of the free was an import. By voting a series of changes in the immigration laws starting in 1924, Congress made a mess of the open-door policy that had made New York and the nation great. By 1929, immigration had been reduced to 150,000 per year allowed, with not nearly that many actually arriving because a nation-of-origin quota system had been established. The quotas favored applicants from Great Britain and northern Europe over applicants from southern and eastern Europe. Italians and Greeks, for example, were forced to wait in line while the absurdly ample British quota—more than 65,000 a year—was not nearly filled. It took forty years for the country to begin to correct the national-quotas injustice with the passage of the 1965 Immigration Act, which went into effect in 1968. Meanwhile, New York State was the poorer for losing much of the diverse immigration that had helped it grow.

17

Normalcy and Beyond

$\mathcal{A}$ Republican newspaper editor from Ohio, Warren G.
Harding, and his running-mate Calvin Coolidge of Massachusetts won the 1920 presidential election. A few months
earlier, addressing a group of Boston businessmen, Harding had
explained his political creed: "America's present need is not
heroics but healing; not nostrums but normalcy; not revolution
but restoration; . . . not surgery but serenity."[1]

New York was ready for normalcy—but insisted on defining
it in accordance with New York visions. The younger generation, disillusioned by the war, was eager to rebel in personal
terms. New Yorkers took to the new, the faddish, and as often
as not the meretricious: roadsters, Mah-Jongg, Eskimo Pies (the
stickless forerunner of the Good Humor), radio, pocket flasks,
cigarettes, Freud, jazz, and tabloid or half-sized newspapers like
the *Daily News,* which was founded in 1919. Movie stars and
sports heroes were elevated to superhuman heights. New York
had a baseball player of extraordinary prowess, a blocky, round-
faced transfer from the Boston Red Sox named George Herman
Ruth, whom the Yankees purchased in 1920. Ruth had been an
excellent pitcher, but he also had an uncanny ability to swat
baseballs into the bleachers for home runs. "Home Run"

1. Quoted in Charles A. and Mary R. Beard, *The Rise of American Civilization,* 2
vols. (New York: The Macmillan Company, 1927, 1946), 2:664.

Baker, the Philadelphia star, had won his nickname for a season's total of twelve home runs. In 1927, four years after the Yankees had built a new stadium in the Bronx (often called "The House that Ruth Built"), the Babe hit sixty home runs—a record that stood until 1961, by which time the season was longer and the baseball livelier.

While seriousness seemed a subject for laughter, the 1920s in New York were marked by an explosion of creative vitality. The New York theater, one of the city's prime attractions for one hundred years, took a remarkable turn for the better. Since the 1890s, New York producers like Erlanger and Klaw and their successors the Shubert brothers, Sam, Lee, and Jacob, had supplied America with theater by dispatching their productions across the land to play every city big enough to raise an audience for a night or two. From a theatrical point of view, the United States was divided in two parts: Broadway and the Road. Big-name stars in star vehicles, however absurd, were the time-proven way to box-office success. Even on Broadway, a serious play on a serious subject by an American playwright was rare.

On February 3, 1920, a play called *Beyond the Horizon* was presented at the Morosco Theater on West Forty-fifth Street. It was a tragedy about two brothers in love with the same girl, and it was the first produced full-length play by a thirty-two-year-old, Eugene O'Neill, who had been born not much more than two blocks away in a hotel at Broadway and Forty-third Street. O'Neill's father, James, had been a great box-office draw of just the kind managers treasured, famous for his portrayal of Edmond Dantes in *The Count of Monte Cristo,* which he had played some six thousand times all over the United States. His son, who was himself handsome enough to be a matinee idol, wanted to be something other than an actor. By 1912, aged twenty-four, he had worked as a reporter on the New London, Connecticut, *Telegraph* but found that newspaper work was not quite right, either. During the next two years, O'Neill wrote five one-act plays and published them at his father's expense in a thin book, *Thirst And Other One-Act Plays.* He gave a copy to Clayton Hamilton, dramatic critic of the *Bookman* magazine. Hamilton helped O'Neill get admitted as a special student to

Professor George F. Baker's famous playwriting course at Harvard, English 47.

In 1915, a group of Greenwich Villagers led by George Cram Cook and his wife, Susan Glaspell, the novelist, started an experimental theater in an old fishery at the end of a wharf in Provincetown, Massachusetts. They called themselves The Provincetown Players and wrote themselves into history in 1916 by putting on O'Neill's one-act play *Bound East for Cardiff.* That fall, the group found a "theater" for themselves in New York, the parlor floor of an old brownstone at 139 MacDougall Street half a block south of Washington Square. There they continued to present new plays—O'Neill's and many others'— mostly to a small band of loyal subscribers. The Washington Square Players, a slightly older and more professional group a few blocks away, also produced one of O'Neill's one-act plays, *In The Zone,* in 1917. (The Washington Square Players, founded in 1914 by Lawrence Langner, Philip Moeller, and several others, were only two years away from turning themselves into The Theatre Guild.)

From one-act plays to three-act plays and from MacDougall Street to the Morosco were two considerable steps forward in O'Neill's career. The producer of *Beyond The Horizon,* John D. Williams, called the first performance a "special matinee" and waited to see what the reaction would be before he committed himself to a theater rental. The audience response was muted— they were quiet because they were moved. Williams and O'Neill had to wait for the reviews, including Alexander Woollcott's in the *Times* and Heywood Broun's in the *Tribune,* to be sure they had a probable success. *Beyond The Horizon* won O'Neill his first Pulitzer Prize. *Anna Christie,* produced a year later, won him his second; *Strange Interlude,* produced in 1928, his third. In 1936 he was awarded the Nobel Prize for literature—the only American playwright who has received it.

O'Neill's success, combined with the excitement many other talents in the theater were engendering, inspired all kinds of first-class work. Not long ago, Harold Clurman, the late writer, director, and theater critic, wrote a piece about the "best" theater season of all time—meaning, as he explained, his favorite.

He chose the 1924–1925 season, which included O'Neill's *Desire Under The Elms* (with a little-known actor, Walter Huston, in the cast); Sidney Howard's *They Knew What They Wanted,* with Pauline Lord; Maxwell Anderson's and Laurence Stalling's *What Price Glory?;* Philip Barry's *The Youngest;* George S. Kaufman's and Marc Connelly's *Beggar On Horseback;* and Ferenc Molnar's *The Guardsman,* starring Alfred Lunt and Lynn Fontanne. It also had George and Ira Gershwin's *Lady Be Good,* with Fred and Adele Astaire; Jeanne Eagles in Somerset Maugham's *Rain;* and Katherine Cornell in George Bernard Shaw's *Candida.* Richard Rodgers and Larry Hart collaborated on *The Garrick Gaieties,* and Cole Porter contributed ten songs to the sixth edition of the *Greenwich Village Follies.* A total of 228 shows opened that season, about five times as many as in 1979–1980.

Creative vitality was by no means confined to the theatrical arts. It was a time for inventing magazines. DeWitt Wallace, an army veteran who had been wounded in the Meuse–Argonne offensive of 1918, had amused himself while recuperating by condensing magazine articles. By 1920, he thought he had an idea for a new magazine: a monthly assemblage, pocket-sized, of the best recent articles from other people's magazines. He called it *Reader's Digest.* Working in his Greenwich Village apartment, Wallace produced a sample with the help of the young social worker he was on the point of marrying, Lila Bell Acheson, and sent it around to publishers, editors, and potential investors. In return Wallace received some compliments but not a penny of invested capital. He borrowed $1,300 and, with his own modest savings, went ahead. He mailed out his first issue in 1921 to 1,500 "subscribers" who were entitled to get their money back if they did not like the magazine.

Luckily, there were hardly any claims. *Reader's Digest* was an immediate success in that sense, but for a time the Wallaces were their own staff. Wallace spent countless hours, in those pre-Xerox days, sitting at the big tables in the Public Library's Periodical Room copying out articles of lasting significance in longhand and condensing as he copied. He would have given the magazine away, Wallace said later, if anyone had offered to take it and put him on salary. Since no one made that offer, Mr. and Mrs. Wallace, sixty years later, were sole owners of by far the most popular magazine in the history of periodical literature: a circulation of 30,000,000—18,000,000 in the United States and 12,000,000 abroad—and thirty-nine editions worldwide published in fifteen different languages. *Reader's Digest* moved to the suburbs long before most corporations considered such a thing, and its headquarters are now in the Westchester County town of Pleasantville.

In 1923 a pair of Yale men, Briton Hadden and Henry R. Luce, started *Time,* the country's first national weekly news-magazine. Like *Reader's Digest, Time* flattered its readers by implying that they were hard-pressed for time. The week's news of the world was compressed, departmentalized, and written in a rapid-fire, mannered style pumped full of eccentricities that seemed, to those who liked its flavor, delightful. As things worked out during the next half-century, *Time* was the first building block in a large, carefully constructed publishing empire. Hadden died an untimely death. In 1930, only a few months after the stock-market crash, Luce launched *Fortune*— an elegant, handsomely designed and illustrated monthly business magazine. In 1936, Time Inc. added *Life,* a picture magazine, to its repertoire. (The old *Life,* a humor magazine, had failed and Luce had bought the rights to its title.) *Sports Illustrated* appeared in 1954. *Life* faltered and folded, presumably a victim like many other magazines of the flight of readers and advertisers' dollars toward television. But *People* and *Money* were founded, and *Life* was reborn as a monthly instead of a weekly. Meanwhile, Time Inc. had reached out into three related fields: book publishing, television, and forest products. It bought the Book-of-the-Month Club, Little, Brown & Company, and the *Washington Star* and started a cable pay-television company, Home Box Office. Diversification, the theory went, should protect the magazines against the vagaries of popular taste, business cycles, and the odious possibility that images on tubes might take the place of print on paper.

Soon after *Time*'s debut—on February 19, 1925, but dated two days later—the first issue of *The New Yorker* magazine appeared. Its cover sported Rea Irwin's drawing of a top-hatted boulevardier of some earlier era gazing imperturbably through his monocle at a pink butterfly. (The same cover runs every year on the anniversary issue.) The magazine was the invention of a thirty-three-year-old perfectionist, Harold W. Ross, who came from Colorado, had worked on a number of newspapers in the Southwest and West, and had been the managing editor of the army's overseas newspaper, *Stars and Stripes,* in Paris. He had imagined *The New Yorker* and several other magazines while editing the *American Legion Monthly* in New York, but like Wallace, Hadden, and Luce, Ross had had his problems raising money. Raoul H. Fleischmann, a member of Ross's group of poker-playing friends, saved the day by investing $25,000. That sum, added to $25,000 of Ross's own, seemed sufficient. (Ross was dreaming. Before *The New Yorker* began to pay for itself, about 1929, Fleischmann had invested an additional $400,000 and had lent the magazine almost that much again.)

For a time the magazine depended too heavily on the styles of *Judge, Life* (which was slipping), and England's *Punch;* yet something about Ross attracted first-class talent like Dorothy Parker, Ring Lardner, E. B. White, Robert Benchley, and Alexander Woollcott. In addition to finding and inspiring contributors, Ross was an innovator. He invented the one line cartoon caption, the "Talk of the Town" story, the "Profile," the "Letter" form epitomized by Janet Flanner's columns from Paris and Mollie Panter-Downes's from London. As Ross's successor, William Shawn, once wrote, all of these were "different in form and intention than anything that had gone before."

Ross had an insatiable hunger for facts, which not only inspired his reporters to hunt for them but led to the establishment of the magazine's famous Checking Department, half a dozen or more young men and women, highly qualified in a variety of languages and disciplines, who spared no effort in an attempt to verify or correct every factual statement in the magazine's text. He was equally passionate about grammar and usage and assembled a large staff of editors to pore over proofs in the vain hope that an error-free issue of a hundred or two hundred pages could be achieved. Ross had originally thought of *The New*

Yorker as a local magazine, more parochial than *Life* or *Judge,* but his brainchild refused to stay at home. Before Ross's death in 1951, the magazine was setting a new standard for journalistic excellence all over the English-speaking world.

By the mid-Twenties, postwar prosperity seemed secure and perhaps destined to continue forever. Some New Yorkers were occupied, happily, watching their stocks go up and thinking of new cocktail recipes to disguise the taste of Prohibition liquor. New York was less sympathetic to Prohibition than was any other state, and anyone who wanted a drink got a drink. Instead of bars there were speakeasies, an estimated 30,000 in the greater New York City area alone, which did business with varying degrees of surreptitiousness.

A man for that season, James A. Walker, aged forty-four, was elected mayor of New York City in 1925. His father, a Democratic party leader, had raised Jimmy on politics—with the result that the son was more interested in almost everything else, including amateur theatricals, piano-playing, song-writing, and dressing in the latest Broadway style. Walker loved show business and the people in it. He had worked for a music publisher and had written the lyrics for "Will You Love Me In December As You Do in May?"—a great hit. He had served in the State Assembly since 1912, representing Tammany to the best of his ability. He seemed debonair, jaunty, devil-may-care; but those who knew him well understood that he was unusually nervous, afraid of crowds and elevators, and constitutionally unable to get anywhere on time. He also told jokes with the skill of a professional stand-up comedian.

He joked about not having gone to college. "What little I know," Walker said, "I have learned by ear." He knew that New York had grave problems: the powerful Board of Estimate ran the city, and jobs, public offices, and favors were sold to the highest bidders; the criminal underworld, which had flourished under Prohibition, moved in on City Hall and on the city's government at every level. When rumors of widespread corruption began to circulate, Jimmy brushed questions aside with wisecracks.

In Albany, Governor Al Smith continued on the opposite tack. He had been born in 1873 on the Lower East Side, next to the construction site of the Brooklyn Bridge, in a slum dominated by first- and second-generation Irish Catholics. His father, a teamster, had died when Al was thirteen. Smith had left school at fifteen to go to work; by the time he was twenty-five he had been a freight clerk, a shipping clerk, a pipe-handler, and a salesman at the Fulton Fish Market, and he had made himself uncommonly useful at his local Democratic club. In 1903, with Tammany backing, Smith was elected to the State Assembly. He was a loyal Tammany man, but during the next twelve years he turned himself into an expert on the theory and practice of the state's government. In 1911, he became majority leader of the Assembly; in 1913, he became its speaker.

In 1918, after serving as the sheriff of New York County (Manhattan) and as president of the New York City Board of Aldermen, Smith was elected governor of New York State. He had developed into a dedicated reformer and a superbly skillful political tactician, and during his four terms—interrupted from 1920 to 1922 by losing the governorship to Nathan Miller— Smith led the legislature to adopt a remarkable body of welfare legislation. When confronted by Republican majorities in both the Senate and the Assembly, Smith outmaneuvered them. He was a great public speaker with a showman's sense of humor. His heavy Lower East Side accent, sprinkled with "deses" and "dozes" and bizarre mispronunciations (he called the radio the "raddio"), was an asset, at least downstate. A preponderance of voters loved to laugh at his manner and support the substance of Smith's appeals. He steadily drew apart from Tammany. When it came to a showdown, Smith was able and willing to prove that the real source of his power was the ballot box.

By the time Smith ran for the presidency in 1928, New York was perhaps the best-run state in the nation. The work week had been cut to forty-eight hours. New safety standards had been established for women and children working in industry. The workmen's compensation law had been revised into the most liberal statute of its kind in the world—Smith's proudest achievement. Hospital, prisons, and bridges had been built; the state's parks and recreational areas had been expanded; and the state was providing aid for county roadbuilding, hospitals, and health facilities.

It is possible that no Democrat could have defeated the Republican presidential nominee, Herbert Hoover, in the midst of the nation's prosperity in 1928—Republican prosperity, according to all Republican party spokesmen. If that was true, the campaign was needlessly savage. Smith was the first Catholic ever nominated, a fact that bigots, addressing other bigots, exploited to the full. Smith, like most New Yorkers, thought the time to repeal the Prohibition Amendment had come; that cost him countless votes in the South and in many small towns and rural areas throughout the nation. He was caricatured as a city slicker, a Tammany hack, and an ignoramus with a funny accent. Hoover's victory was overwhelming: he carried forty of the forty-eight states and won by 444 votes to 87 in the Electoral College. Smith had failed to reach the one political goal he wanted the most.

Not quite a year later, after a few warning tremors, the stock market collapsed. Opening prices on October 24, 1929—known ever since as Black Thursday—were steady enough, but the rate at which shares were being bought and sold was unusually high, and the ticker tape could not keep up. At the end of an hour it was evident that prices were falling, and fast. By November 13, when the market hit bottom for the year, billions of dollars in paper profits had disappeared—never before, or since, have prices declined so fast or so far. Prosperity had begun to fade in early 1929; iron and steel production were down, along with automobile output and building. But speculative mania, much of it fueled by borrowed money, had glossed over that reality and many others. The break in the bull market, which was five years old, signaled an oncoming depression that turned out to be deeper and longer-lived than even the economic pessimists could imagine.

18

Contemplating 2000

$\mathcal{A}$S New York entered the final decades of the twentieth century, its citizens were optimistic in their characteristically guarded way. Those who could remember as far back as the Great Depression—or who had read history—knew that when the appalling collapse of the state's, the nation's, and to a considerable extent the world's economies occurred, New York had been fortunate enough to have two capable executives in Albany, Governor Franklin D. Roosevelt and Lieutenant Governor Herbert H Lehman.

Roosevelt, in 1928, had been Governor Smith's choice. The new administration was pledged to complete the development programs Smith had begun, and it tried to do so. Governor Roosevelt gathered together a remarkable group of aides and advisers to help him: Louis McHenry Howe, James A. Farley, Frances Perkins, Samuel I. Rosenman, Harry Hopkins, Henry Morgenthau, Jr., and some of the members of what was later called the "Brain Trust," including Rexford G. Tugwell, A. A. Berle, Jr., and Raymond Moley. Within months after the stock-market crash Roosevelt started to help New York's unemployed with emergency relief and temporary public works jobs. He was one of the first of the nation's government officials to realize that the economic disaster made joblessness a public, governmental responsibility—a problem far too great for private charity. (By 1932, half of the males in New York State were unemployed or working only part time.) After Roosevelt's election to the presidency, Governor Lehman, Roosevelt's close friend, carried on. For ten remarkable years, from 1932 to 1942, Lehman guided New York's "Little New Deal" with dignity and administrative acumen that made the horrendous task seem almost effortless.

Old New Yorkers might also recall that in 1933, after Mayor Walker had resigned in disgrace, caught out by Judge Samuel Seabury's searching investigation into City Hall corruption, New York City voters had the wit to elect an extraordinary multilingual reform Republican named Fiorello La Guardia. On his first day in office, Mayor La Guardia took to the radio to read the pledge that young men of ancient Athens took when they were old enough to become citizens. It ended: "we will strive to transmit this city not less but greater, better, and more beautiful than it was transmitted to us." La Guardia's word was as good as any Athenian's. He was a magician at persuading the federal government to pour money into New York's job-creating projects: a new subway for Sixth Avenue; a new tunnel under the East River, connecting midtown Manhattan with Queens; completion of the Triborough Bridge; roads, schools, hospitals, libraries, parks, swimming pools; and an airport at the mouth of Flushing Bay. His own ebullience helped too: the story of his reading the comics over the radio during one of New York City's periodic newspaper strikes is now a legend.

All but the youngest New Yorkers could remember the time when there had been more New Yorkers. The state's population stopped growing after 1970, when it reached 18,200,000. In the middle 1960s, the largest-population championship passed to California. The population of New York City also has dwindled, from 7,900,000 in 1970 to about 7,200,000 in 1980 (the precise size of the shrinkage is vague, in part because numbers of illegal aliens live and work in New York and prefer not to talk to census takers or anyone else who resembles, however faintly, The Law).

New York's growth has been stunted, partly by the well-publicized upper-middle-class flight to the suburbs and partly by the sharp curtailment of immigration in 1924. On the other hand, it has been stimulated by the migration of Southern blacks into the city before and after World War I and by Puerto Ricans starting on the eve of World War II. By 1965, there were 1,200,000 blacks in the city, more in Brooklyn than in Harlem, and perhaps 400,000 in all the rest of the state. A substantial number of Puerto Ricans have been importees, rather than immigrants; they were talked into moving by agents for New York employers, especially garment-industry manufacturers, who needed unskilled workers because the war absorbed manpower, skilled and unskilled, at an unprecedented rate. Employment in Puerto Rico was sagging. And numbers of Puerto Ricans had no particular objection to doing menial, unpleasant jobs behind the scenes in New York hotels and restaurants, for one example. Daily airline flights from San Juan, with tickets paid for by a New York City employer, made the leap from one society to another quick and easy. By 1960, the census indicated, there were 612,000 Puerto Ricans in the city. By 1970 there were 963,000; and although numbers of Puerto Ricans as well as blacks were counter-migrating during the 1970s, there was little doubt that an additional decade had brought a considerable net increase in both populations.

Those New Yorkers who were downcast by the overall population shrinkage were likely to explain that geographical boundary lines had lost some significance, although not politically. The true New York City, they would argue, really includes all those men and women who sleep in New Jersey and Connecticut and Westchester and Rockland counties but earn their livings in the city. By that criterion, reminiscent of the Dutch West India Company's claim, New York deserves credit for an additional couple of million. In fact, within New York State itself the city's immediate influence reaches at least into Dutchess County, or well over 100 miles to the north.

Those who remembered that New York had lost hundreds of thousands of manufacturing jobs during the 1970s could console themselves with the fact that New York State remains the nation's leader in the production of manufactured goods. The list of things includes wearing apparel, food products, machinery, chemicals, paper, electrical equipment (Schenectady's specialty), and cameras (Rochester remains famous for them). If New York is second, after Wisconsin, as a milk producer, it is first in the production of timothy, maple syrup, cream cheese, and creamed cottage cheese. If it is only third in the manufacture of ice cream, lagging behind California and Pennsylvania, it regularly leads all the other states in the production of zinc, talc, titanium, and emery. If it is second in apple-growing, after Washington, New York has more institutions of higher learning—285—than any other state, and the highest per-pupil expenditure in its public schools—$2,645, almost double the national average.

New York City became the unofficial capital of the world, the home of the United Nations Organization, after World War II by providing twenty-odd acres of Manhattan along the East River as international territory. John D. Rockefeller, Jr., at the suggestion of his son Nelson, bought the property for $8,500,000 and gave it to the United Nations. (If he had not done so, Philadelphia might be the unofficial capital of the world.)

New York had already become—unofficially, again—the world capital of the arts. A number of abstract expressionist painters, with Jackson Pollock at their forefront and including Arshile Gorky, Mark Rothko, Robert Motherwell, and Willem de Kooning among others, were seen to constitute a "New York School" of painting, and New York replaced Paris as the center of the international *avant-garde*. George Balanchine, born in St. Petersburg in 1904, came to New York in 1933. He was one of the founders, the following year, of the School of American Ballet, and as a choreographer he helped formulate what was known around the world as the "American style" of classical ballet. Balanchine directed the New York City Ballet from its beginning, in 1948.

The Metropolitan Opera had been thinking of building a new house since 1908, and by the late 1950s the Philharmonic was desperate to find a new home because Carnegie Hall's landlord was going to tear it down. (It was subsequently reprieved.) The idea of pulling New York's cultural institutions together in one place had long been in the air—La Guardia, among others, had suggested it—and it came to pass under the leadership of John D. Rockefeller, 3rd. Fifteen acres of land were cleared just west and south of the intersection of Broadway and Columbus Avenue at Sixty-fifth Street. President Dwight D. Eisenhower turned over the first spadeful of earth in the ground-breaking ceremonies on May 14, 1959. The Metropolitan Opera, the Philharmonic, the New York City Ballet, the New York City Opera, the Lincoln Center Repertory Theater, Juilliard School, and the Public Library's Museum and Library of the Performing Arts waited impatiently for the completion of their new homes. Philharmonic Hall (which later became Avery Fisher Hall) was the first building completed, in 1962, and by that time the American "cultural explosion" (which has not yet stopped reverberating) was gathering force. Lincoln Center for the Performing Arts became a model for cultural centers all over the United States, and even abroad. (Some of them learned, in time, that building auditoria is much easier than building a cluster of first-class performing institutions.)

While some might say that culture is its own reward, there are benefits on the side, too. By 1980, tourism had become New York State's second largest industry, after manufactures. Its cultural institutions, along with the Statue of Liberty, the United Nations, Niagara Falls, and the World Trade Center, were central to the decision-making of millions of travellers. They chose New York as their destination rather than someplace else, and that, in a year, brought $3,500,000,000 into the state. Leaving commercial theater aside, New York State was the home of more than one thousand well-established non-profit arts institutions—orchestras and choruses, opera and ballet companies, museums, galleries, theaters, schools. They employed some 400,000 people and generated half a billion dollars' worth of activity, primarily admissions. According to the chairman of the board of Lincoln Center, Amyas Ames, for every dollar spent on tickets another $1.40 is spent on hotels, restaurants, parking, and the like—all subject to New York taxes.

Nelson Rockefeller was elected governor in 1958, defeating the Democratic incumbent, W. Averell Harriman, and served for fifteen years. Governor Rockefeller, as much as any man,

helped the arts revolution. He became a trustee of the Metropolitan Museum of Art in 1930, the year he was graduated Phi Beta
Kappa from Dartmouth College; he spent a major part of his life
collecting primitive and modern art; he founded the Museum of
Primitive Art in 1957, partly to provide space for his own collection. Rockefeller was extremely knowledgeable about painting and sculpture, and furthermore he loved it. He filled the
governor's mansion with cubist and abstract expressionist work;
if some legislative leaders were bewildered, from the painters'
point of view the exposure was a delight. The governor pressed
the legislature to approve a $15,000,000 contribution to Lincoln
Center to help pay for the New York State Theater, where the
City Ballet and the City Opera perform. He urged dramatic
increases in the budget for the State Council on the Arts, which
allocates money to non-profit institutions throughout the state.
The appropriation rose to $32,000,000—not nearly enough,
Rockefeller felt, and yet that sum was equal to all the other
states' support for the arts added together.

Rockefeller's enthusiasm for education was almost as great as
his interest in art. He recast the state's university system. The
number of campuses increased from twenty-eight to seventy-
one, the number of students enrolled from 38,000 to 246,000.
The governor increased state aid to private universities, state aid
to local school districts, and the number and amount of state
scholarships to both public and private schools.

Rockefeller transformed downtown Albany by clearing a
space for a gigantic $1,500,000,000 Empire State Mall (now the
Nelson A. Rockefeller Plaza), a complex of towering glass-
and-marble state office buildings rising over a long plaza that
connects the old State House with the massive new State
Museum. His critics fussed and fumed about extravagance; but
there were few, after the project was finished, who were not
proud of its noble conception. The bills for the mall and all the
other Rockefeller improvements were, of course, high. During
his fifteen years in office, the state budget quadrupled: state
taxes, per person, rose from $94 to $460 a year on the average;
and the stste's debt was four times greater than it had been. But
when Rockefeller resigned in 1973—it was assumed that he was

getting ready to run for the presidency for the fourth time, but instead he was eventually appointed vice president by President Ford—the New York State budget was a mere $8,850,000,000 as contrasted with $14,000,000,000 in 1980.

As often as not, in New York's history, the newcomers—of whom there have always been an abundance—have evaluated the place with great accuracy. The summer of 1977 was a time to try the patience of anyone. New York City was in its fourth year of serious financial crisis, with the possibility of bankruptcy far from dismissed. An electric power failure, the second serious one in twelve years, blacked out New York City and revived doubts about whether the engineers understood how the power system worked. During a night of darkness, an appalling amount of looting and senseless property destruction took place. Six months later, the *New York Times* and the Columbia Broadcasting System conducted an extensive public-opinion poll in an effort to find out what New Yorkers thought about their city and how they imagined the future would be. There were optimists and pessimists of all races, religions, and national backgrounds, but blacks and Puerto Ricans, especially those who lived in Manhattan and the Bronx, were significantly more hopeful about New York's future than were New Yorkers as a whole. For that matter, the entire sample was anything but defeated: the majority believed that in ten or fifteen years New York would be a better place to live. A second question, which required no forecasting talent, may have been a sign that the optimistic majority was right. Four out of five New Yorkers questioned—a landslide result—were "proud to say" that they lived in New York.

New York's diversity in all things, including the national, ethnic, religious, and cultural differences that separated the first colonists—the things the Walloons must have said about the Dutch!—is its secret. Not that diversity, in itself, has any particular value one way or another. Diversity, taken for granted, allows almost any kind of talent to try itself, to succeed, or fail, or waffle some place in between, without unnecessary comment or concern on the part of the community. New Yorkers have never accepted the proposition—I should say, instead, that few have done so—that the state would be enhanced by a monochromatic society of people who worship and dream exactly like everyone else. It is lucky that diversity is not an issue that the New York Assembly and the New York Senate could put to a vote since it might be tabled. Presumably, diversity would be defeated, temporarily, while a state investigative commission looked into the question of what might constitute conformity, from a legal point of view.

Happily, New York's secret is safe.

Suggestions for Further Reading

My system for choosing these few books from the vast number that have been written about New York is simple: I like them. Some are books to read, some are books to look things up in, some are both. In one way or another, I've needed them all in writing this book.

Robert G. Albion. *The Rise of New York Port, 1815–1860*. New York: Charles Scribner's Sons, 1970.

Charles M. Andrews. *The Colonial Background of the American Revolution*. New Haven, Conn.: Yale University Press, 1931.

Charles A. and Mary R. Beard. *The Rise of American Civilization*. New York: The Macmillan Co., 1946.

Meyer Berger. *Meyer Berger's New York*. New York: Random House, 1960.

Bruce Bliven, Jr. *Battle for Manhattan*. New York: Henry Holt & Co., 1956.

Bruce Bliven, Jr. *Under the Guns: New York 1775–1776*. New York: Harper & Row, 1972.

Carl Bridenbaugh. *Cities in Revolt: Urban Life in America 1743–1776*. New York: Alfred A. Knopf, 1955.

Carl Carmer. *The Tavern Lamps are Burning*. New York: David McKay, 1964.

Carl Carmer. *The Hudson*. Revised edition. New York: Grosset & Dunlap, 1968.

George Dangerfield. *Chancellor Robert R. Livingston of New York 1746–1813*. New York: Harcourt, Brace & Co., 1960.

Marshall B. Davidson. *New York: A Pictorial History*. New York: Charles Scribner's Sons, 1977.

Elmer Davis. *History of the New York Times 1851–1921*. New York: Greenwood Press, 1921.

David M. Ellis, James A. Frost, Harold C. Syrett, and Harry J. Carman. *A History of New York State*. Ithaca, N.Y.: Cornell University Press, 1967.

Douglas Southall Freeman. *George Washington: A Biography.* 7 vols. New York: Charles Scribner's Sons, 1948–1957.

James T. Flexner. *History of American Painting.* 3 vols. New York: Dover Books, 1962.

James T. Flexner. *Young Hamilton: A Biography.* Boston: Little, Brown & Co., 1978.

Alexander C. Flick, editor. *History of the State of New York.* 10 vols. New York: Columbia University Press, 1937.

Nathan Glazer and Daniel P. Moynihan. *Beyond the Melting Pot.* Cambridge, Mass.: Massachusetts Institute of Technology and Harvard University Press, 1963.

Michael G. Kammen. *Colonial New York: A History.* New York: Charles Scribner's Sons, 1975.

John A. Kouwenhoven. *The Columbia Historical Portrait of New York.* New York: Doubleday & Co., 1953.

Susan E. Lyman. *The Story of New York.* New York: Crown Publishers, 1964.

John C. Miller. *Origins of the American Revolution.* Boston: Little, Brown & Co., 1943.

Lloyd Morris. *Incredible New York.* New York: Random House, 1951.

New York: A Guide to the Empire State. New York: Oxford University Press, 1941.

V. S. Pritchett. *New York Proclaimed.* New York: Harcourt, Brace & World, 1965.

Kate Simon. *Fifth Avenue: A Very Social History.* New York: Harcourt, Brace, Jovanovich, 1978.

Alfred E. Smith. *Up to Now: An Autobiography.* New York: Viking Press, 1929.

I. N. P. Stokes. *The Iconography of Manhattan Island, 1498–1909.* 6 vols. New York: R. H. Dodd, 1915–1928; reissued, New York: Arno Press, 1967.

Henri and Barbara Van der Zee. *A Sweet and Alien Land: The Story of Dutch New York.* New York: Viking Press, 1978.

Christopher Ward. *The War of the Revolution.* 2 vols. New York: The Macmillan Co., 1952.

M. R. Werner. *Tammany Hall.* Second edition. New York: Greenwood Press, 1968.

James G. Wilson, editor. *The Memorial History of New York.* 2 vols. New York: New-York History Co., 1892.

Index

189